FACE TO FACE

BECOMING
A HAPPIER MARRIED COUPLE

BY
GABRIEL CALVO

Face To Face

ISBN: 0-936098-57-0

Edited by: Kathy Kelley

Illustrations by: Christine Krueger

CONTENTS

THIS BOOK IS
DEDICATED
TO
ALL
MARRIED COUPLES
WHO ARE WILLING
TO
SEARCH THEIR HEARTS
FOR ALL THAT IS
WITHIN THEM.

MAY YOUR PATHS
BE BLESSED
WITH HOPE AND JOY.

ACKNOWLEDGEMENT

THANK YOU

From The Bottom Of My Heart

To:

. . . **The Hundreds Of Married Couples** from Spain, Italy, Ireland, England, France, Latin America, United States, Canada, Africa, Philippines and Japan, who, through their written and lived experiences have inspired me, and have enriched this book in a very special way.

. . . **Tom and Trudy Ryan** for their dedicated coordination of the "Marriage Encounter At Home" FIRES Program, which was the core of this book.

. . . **All The People Who Will Read This Book** and, afterwards, will send me a note, testimonial letter, or a brief report about their progress.

. . . **To Everyone Who Will Read This Book With An Open Mind And Open Heart.**

FOREWORD

THIS IS NOT JUST A BOOK,
IT IS A WORKBOOK.
YOU ARE INVITED NOT TO JUST READ IT,
BUT TO EXPERIENCE IT.

THIS BOOK IS NOT ABOUT MARRIAGE,
BUT FOR MARRIED COUPLES.
IT IS BASED NOT SO MUCH ON THEORETICAL IDEAS
   OR PRINCIPLES BUT ON THE LIVED EXPERIENCES
   OF SO MANY MARRIED COUPLES, WHO, AFTER ALL,
   ARE THE REAL EXPERTS ON MARRIAGE AND
   FAMILY LIFE.

IT IS AN OPPORTUNITY FOR MARRIED COUPLES
TO GROW AS HEALTHY AND HAPPY COUPLES.

MARRIAGE IS AN ONGOING PROCESS
BASED ON A CONTINUOUSLY DEVELOPING RELATIONSHIP.
YOUR EXPERIENCE IS NEVER PERFECT OR COMPLETE.
YOU CAN NEVER SPEAK OF YOUR MARRIAGE AS A
   PAST EVENT
BECAUSE YOU ARE CALLED TO BECOME MARRIED
   EVERY DAY.
A WEDDING IS A ONCE AND FOR ALL AFFAIR, BUT
   MARRIAGE CAN BE RE-LIVED WITH NEW FRESHNESS
   EACH DAY.

TODAY, WHEN THERE IS SO MUCH TALK ABOUT
   MARRIAGE BREAKDOWN, MILLIONS OF MARRIED
   COUPLES ARE SEARCHING WITH GREAT HOPE FOR
   FULFILLMENT AND HAPPINESS IN THEIR MARRIED LIFE.
ARE YOU ONE OF THOSE?

FOR THIS VERY REASON I HAVE TRIED TO DRAW ON
   THE **LIVED EXPERIENCES** OF MEN AND WOMEN,
   FRIENDS OF MINE, WHO IN SPITE OF THE
   PRESSURES — BOTH INTERNAL AND EXTERNAL —
   ARE MAKING A SUCCESS OF THEIR MARRIAGE AND
   FAMILY LIFE.
WITHOUT THE LIVED EXPERIENCES OF THESE
   COUPLES, IT WOULD NOT HAVE BEEN POSSIBLE TO
   WRITE THIS BOOK.
BUT THIS BOOK IS INCOMPLETE.
YOU CAN COMPLETE IT BY EXPERIENCING AND
   SHARING IT.

INTRODUCTION

In March of 1986, we went away with Father Calvo for a long weekend to update the FIRES "Marriage Encounter At Home" manual. We feel blessed to have been working with Father Calvo since 1981 as coordinators of this program.

That weekend was an intense, fun, growing, draining and spiritually uplifting experience. Working with Father Calvo is never dull. Near the end of the weekend, he had an inspiration. Incidentally, it doesn't take a special weekend for Father Calvo to have an inspiration; we believe that's his middle name.

His inspiration, he shared with us, was that rather than updating the M.E. At Home Workbook, he dreamt instead of writing a book that could reach all couples. Thus the first seed for this book began to sprout.

Father Calvo started Marriage Encounter in Barcelona, Spain in 1962. At that time he spent a Weekend with 28 working-class couples who experienced the first M.E. Since then, millions of couples all over the world have learned to communicate better and grow as individuals and couples, as a result of this weekend experience.

Father Calvo was very aware, though, that:
1. Not all couples could get away to attend a weekend, and,
2. Individuals and families, not just couples, needed practical effective ways to become more fulfilled.

Because of this dream to reach out to every home on earth, to every culture, race and creed, in 1976 he founded FIRES: Family Intercommunications Relationships Experiences Services. FIRES offers individuals, couples and families opportunities to grow in love and unity.

In addition to FIRES, Father Calvo recognized the need for a book which would be readily available to everyone and could help individuals, couples and families reverse the downward spiral in our present-day way of life. **Face to Face** encapsulates the wisdom, humor, love and truth of his 35 years of working with, and ministering to, individuals, couples and families. We're grateful to have helped Father Calvo in this endeavor.

We urge you to not only read this book, but to experience it in depth, day by day. The questions and exercises in the book will assist you.

This book can be used in many ways. For example:
1. **An individual** can grow and benefit from it. A dear friend of ours worked through the exercises by herself. She was able to change, and grow to the point where she was reunited with, and

11

eventually remarried, her former husband.

2. **A couple** can experience the dynamics of the Marriage Encounter Weekend by reading, reflecting and sharing on the questions and exercises in the book. Since this takes place over a longer period of time, the results can be even more dramatic and longer lasting than those experienced during a weekend.

3. The book is also a perfect follow-up to a Marriage Encounter weekend.

4. **A group of couples** can use this book as a study guide for sharing. We did this with six other couples and found it to be a very stimulating and enriching experience for everyone.

Tom and Trudy Ryan.

Where
Are
We?

First Week

WHERE ARE WE?

First Day **LONGING FOR HAPPINESS IN MARRIAGE**

Second Day **BEING A COUPLE**

Third Day **FACING MARRIAGE REALITY**

Fourth Day **DISCOVERING MARRIAGE POTENTIAL**

Fifth Day **IDENTIFYING MARRIAGE NEEDS**

Sixth Day **DISCERNING CONJUGAL LOVE**

Seventh Day **FINDING QUALITY TIME TOGETHER**

"It Is Better To Encounter Today Than To Separate Tomorrow."

Marriage Encounter
Original Manual

WHAT IS HAPPENING
IN YOUR MARRIAGE?

YOUR MARRIAGE
IS NOT JUST A CONCEPT,
IT IS A REALITY.

YOUR MARRIAGE
IS NOT A STATIC REALITY,
IT IS A SOURCE OF TREMENDOUS
POTENTIAL TO CHANGE, TO GROW
AND TO IMPROVE.

YOUR MARRIAGE
IS NOT A PROBLEM TO BE SOLVED,
IT IS A MYSTERIOUS JOURNEY OF
TWO, TOWARD A PROMISED LAND
CALLED "HAPPINESS."

THEREFORE:

STOP COMPLAINING ABOUT YOUR PAST:
THAT BELONGS TO YESTERDAY.
DO NOT WORRY ABOUT YOUR FUTURE:
IT WILL BE REAL TOMORROW.
CONCENTRATE ON YOUR PRESENT, YOUR
TODAY AND YOUR NOW.

BECAUSE:

MARRIAGE IS WHAT YOU MAKE OF IT, NOW!

LONGING FOR
HAPPINESS IN MARRIAGE

Human life is a search for happiness.
The thirst for happiness is in the depth of our beings.
Happiness is everybody's goal in life.

Do happy marriages exist?
We live in an unhappy society. In this world, is it
really possible to have a happy marriage?

Unhappy marriages are one of the world's major evils.
Marriage should be a blessing,
but in many houses it is a curse.

Definitely, staying happily married
Is an art to be learned.

If you read this book along with your spouse
and share it,
You will learn the art of married happiness.

HAPPINESS

Everybody speaks about happiness:

"I am happy." "I am unhappy." "I want to be happy."

"I do not believe in happiness." "Happiness is a myth."

"I do believe in happiness, but I also think that most times, we search for it where it is not."

What is happiness all about?

We do not have a good definition of what it is. We just have descriptions like:

— A general feeling of well-being.

— A sense of satisfaction with your life and work.

— A momentary sensation of euphoria.

It is knowing satisfaction because a desire has been fulfilled.

— It is something that happens while doing something you believe in. Happiness isn't something you do or aim at.

— Happiness is what you are longing for. The fulfillment of what you are seeking.

— A kind of peaceful joy within yourself.

— The acceptance of one's own weakness is the first step for happiness.

Happiness is possible for everyone.

But happiness is not something that occurs like magic. It cannot be acquired once and for all in life. Happiness is intertwined with effort and struggle. Its search is certainly an art.

There is no such thing as a recipe or a secret formula for happiness. But there are some conditions of life that go along with the pursuit of happiness, like self-knowledge, self-esteem, self-discipline and faithfulness to your conscience.

The single most important key for happiness is having an intimate and loving relationship with at least one other person.

Happiness has its enemies, like: the strong emphasis on easy success; immediate gratification; instant pleasure. But the single greatest cause of unhappiness is self-centeredness and excessive preoccupation with self.

17

HAPPINESS IN MARRIAGE

Is happiness possible in marriage, or is it an impossible dream?

Fairy tales about princes and princesses usually end with, "They got married and lived happily ever after."

Is that the true story of every man and woman undertaking marriage?

According to researchers, modern marriages last considerably less than "forever." In 40 per-cent of all marital unions, "I Do" dissolves into "I Don't," "I Can't," or "I Won't."

Yet for every marriage which crumbles, another endures. Many of the longest running relationships not only survive, but thrive through the years. What's the secret?

Scholars and successfully married couples agree that the key to happiness in marriage lies in being aware of your desires and expectations about yourself, your spouse and your marriage relationship.

From that awareness you will have to discern which of those desires are realistic and which are not.

Finally, you will be able to accept only the realistic ones and put to rest your old and foolish longings and wants.

Once you have limited your desires to that which is real, you will find right within your married life the happiness you hoped to find elsewhere.

Therefore, happiness in marriage is possible, but takes real work together, day by day. Marriage cannot make anyone "happier" who does not bring the ingredients for happiness into it.

What are those ingredients?

There is no magical formula for making marriage happier, but you can identify the common characteristics of those happily married couples who become even happier.

How do happily married people think and act?

They . . .

. . . are personally honest with themselves.

. . . firmly believe in their marriage potential.

. . . are seriously committed to making their marriage work.

. . . are mutually open and ready to share their whole self.

. . . courageously face their marriage crises, conflicts and problems together.

. . . know how to handle resentment, anger and jealousy wisely.

. . . mutually trust each other as best friends.

. . . sincerely accept each other as they are and for what they are.

. . . wholeheartedly forgive each other as soon as they need reconciliation.

. . . periodically spend quality time having fun together.

. . . faithfully relate to God as individuals and as a couple.

. . . are constantly open, hospitable and reaching out.

What can you do to become one of those happily married couples? How do you go about it?

The purpose of this book is to help the two of you become a happier couple.

Therefore:

1. KEEP READING day by day.

2. LISTEN to the testimonies with your heart.

3. THINK about the questions.

4. WRITE your answers in a notebook.

5. SHARE with your spouse as much as possible.

6. PRAY TOGETHER with confidence and hope.

7. SUPPORT each other to keep working on the book.

You will then experience the enormous Energy of Love that is dormant in you.

Maybe you will realize what Antonio Machado, a Spanish poet sings:

"I THOUGHT THE FIRE WAS OUT IN MY FIREPLACE.
I STIRRED THE ASHES,
AND I BURNED MY HANDS. . ."

TESTIMONIES

WHAT POSITIVE SIGNS ARE THERE THAT WE HAVE A HAPPY MARRIAGE?

- "We love to be together."
- "We are good friends."
- "We trust and respect each other."
- "We look for the positive things in each other rather than the negative."

- "We affirm and support one another."
- "We both have a deep desire for a better marriage."
- "Our communication is quite good, and we know we've only scratched the surface."
- "We take prime time, each day, to share as a couple."
- "After 12 years of marriage, we still feel and demonstrate a genuine respect and admiration for each other. All the differences between us and all the times we have been a source of disappointment and irritation to one another, have not destroyed the loving respect we feel for one another."

HOW TO HAVE A HAPPIER MARRIAGE?

- "Take more time to communicate and share."
- "Spend more time working and relaxing together."
- "Listen to each other's needs with the heart."
- "Accept each other as each one really is."
- "Emphasize our difference less, and our common goals more."
- "Reveal more of oneself by sharing one's vulnerabilities, fears and frustrations, as well as one's assets."
- "Doing less and being more."
- "Listen and share God's Words."
- "Pray together."

QUESTIONS FOR REFLECTION

THINK about the following questions. They are like a menu. Use your notebook to write on the ones you like the most.

1. *What does it mean to me to be happy in marriage?*
2. *Do I think we have a happy marriage?*
3. *Why did I get married to you?*
4. *Do I think we communicate well?*
5. *Do I accept our differences?*
6. *Do I respect and admire you?*
7. *Do I trust you?*
8. *Do I affirm and support you?*
9. *Do our sexual relations express my love?*
10. *When we offend each other, do I ask and give forgiveness?*
11. *Do I think God is alive in our relationship?*
12. *What can I do to make our marriage happier?*

The
Second Day

BEING A COUPLE

The Wedding was beautiful.
She was resplendent in her gorgeous wedding gown.
He cut a dashing figure in his fancy tux.
Standing in front of the altar, before the white-robed clergy, they
    swore their eternal love for each other.
Three years later they were divorced.
What Happened?
They got married with the firm purpose to be a "couple."
After three years, they realized they were not a couple, but two
    "married singles."
This story is typical of our times.
Every day, thousands of married people, first, blame their spouse for
    lack of understanding, incompatibility or irreconcilable differ-
    ences. Then, after hiring their lawyer to divide up their proper-
    ties, they make custody arrangements and establish separate
    households.
That's the legal divorce.
Why do people get divorced?
What is the innermost root of "legal" divorce?

SPIRITUAL DIVORCE

Legal divorce is the final stage of a long and subtle process. At the root of legal divorce, the one sanctioned by the courts, there is another kind of divorce. It is invisible, personal, and develops hidden from view, inside the married man and woman. We could call it **spiritual divorce,** because it takes place within the persons.

What is spiritual divorce all about? It is a subtle phenomenon marked by a progressive lack of intimacy between husband and wife. It is a mental and emotional divorce. A man and a woman are legally married, remain in the same house, but lead separate lives. They are strangers to one another. Their ideas and emotions no longer seem to connect.

Instead of having concern and feelings for one another that stimulate the growth of their marriage, their lives are fixed on things outside of marriage. A man may invest himself mentally and emotionally in his job, sports or friends. A woman may do the same. Both may even become involved in separate, but worthwhile, causes.

In a legal divorce, the change is external, obvious and dramatic: man and woman no longer live together. In spiritual divorce, the change is not obvious. It is internal and invisible, while they remain physically together. Spiritual divorce usually begins subtly. It can sneak into the best of marriages. It can build gradually through an individualistic mentality, attitude and behavior.

Spiritual divorce could be described as an invisible wall between husband and wife. It is a spiritual cancer that kills marriage and family life.

How can we deal with this dangerous illness in marriage? I would suggest, first, by diagnosing its symptoms, and second, by finding its causes.

IDENTIFYING THE SYMPTOMS OF SPIRITUAL DIVORCE IN YOUR MARRIAGE

To assist you in this important quest, following is a list of some symptoms or signs:
— A deep feeling of isolation and loneliness on the part of either or both of you.
— Almost habitual sadness, disillusion, boredom and emptiness.
— Feelings of dissatisfaction and frustration about the partner.
— Indifference to each other's concerns and problems.

— Coldness in your relationship; lack of sweetness and small courtesies, lack of tenderness such as hugs and kisses.
— Frequent tension and bad temper. Mutual aggressiveness.
— Climate of insincerity and mutual distrust. More confidence in third persons than in your spouse.
— Feelings of fear and insecurity.
— Avoiding or refusing sexual relations.
— Lack of intimate communication and dialogue.
— Frequent quarrels: in your bedroom. . .. in front of your children. . .. everywhere.
— Lack of mutual respect: insults, rude words, ridicule, frequent irony, sarcasm.
— Superficial relationships and continuous escapes: liquor, drugs, vices.
— Individualistic lives: lots of "I" and "Mine;" few of "We," "Ours," "Us."
— Failure to take time to think, enjoy and pray together.
— Lack of faith and hope in your married life.

FINDING THE CAUSES OF YOUR SPIRITUAL DIVORCE

Like the good physician, you cannot feel satisfied just knowing the symptoms. You need to go beyond and find the causes.

According to the experts in marriage communication, lack of understanding in basic areas of marriage is the main root of legal divorce. Therefore, to prevent or to overcome spiritual divorce in your marriage, you need to reach out to understand each other, and find those areas your spouse desires to deal with.

Understanding is gaining new insight into the person of your partner and learning to respect him or her as a person who is different from, yet complementary to you. Understanding is the result of a process of listening and sharing with each other.

To help you on this difficult but very important search, here is a list of some basic areas to reach out to each other and bridge the separation.

HEALTH: Fatigue, nerves, tensions, stress, illnesses. Eating and sleeping habits.

MONEY: Use, abuse, lack of, excess, thoughts, feelings, attitudes, intentions and plans.

TIME:	Meaning, spending, wasting, schedules, priorities, planning.
WORK:	Hers, his; purpose, goals, intentions and desires, reviews.
REST:	Ways to relax; playing, vacationing, hobbies.
NEEDS:	His, hers, as a married couple.
VALUES:	Hers, his, as a married couple.
SEXUAL RELATIONS:	Education, meaning, knowledge, needs, priorities, harmony, self-control.
MARRIED LIFE:	Happiness and unhappiness; love, faith and hopes; challenges, opportunities, changes and growth.
	Common needs and common values.
	Potential and possibilities.
	Limitations.
	Dreams, goals and priorities.
	Successes and failures.
	Plans. . .
CHILDREN:	Each one of them: love, discipline, balance, example, information and education, freedom and responsibility, communication and dialogue.
	Their needs and their values. Their limitations. Their expectations and their frustrations. Their faith, their hopes and their love. Their concerns, their agreements and their disagreements. Their crises.
	Their vocation, their studies and their jobs. Their potential.

24

RELATIVES: Their influence, their problems and concerns.
Their needs and values. Their requests.
Our communication with them.

GOD: Faith, hope, relationships and communication with God.
God's Plan; Word; Will.
Worship, commitment and outreach.

HOME: Atmosphere, intimacy and hospitality.

DEATH: Thoughts, feelings, attitudes, fears and wishes.

TESTIMONIES

BETH   "The lack of romance and adventure in our lives and the consequent feelings of boredom and emptiness which ensue, have been the biggest sign of spiritual divorce in our lives so far.

When I am feeling bored, unappreciated or misunderstood, my first inclination is to find some kind of escape and to imagine myself somewhere else doing something exciting. Another of my favorite escapes from boredom is to fill up my life with busy work. I'm always rushing around trying to get "caught up" but I never seem to get "caught up." Our sideboard remains perpetually crowded with bills to be paid, shopping lists, letters to answer, phone calls that should have been made two weeks ago, mending to be done, etc.

After running around all day, I'm often too exhausted in the evening to enjoy Ed's company or be responsive to his needs. And when his need is to make love, I sometimes view this as one more thing I have to do before I can finally rest my weary bones. I feel guilty when I view our relationship in this way. If I say "yes" to Ed I feel phony. If I say "no," I feel guilty for depriving him of something he needs from me."

ED   "A symptom of spiritual divorce for me is to use sex to affirm our bond when Beth and I are not regularly communicating our feelings. The less communication there is between us, the more I depend on sex. But when we are not close to one another in the communication of our feelings and attitudes, Beth has very little interest in having sex with me. She tolerates my requests for intercourse during those times and I feel resentful and threatened. If we do have intercourse during those times when feelings are not being shared, it is mechanical and lacks spontaneity.

We have found that frequent communication of our feelings and attitudes has reduced the tensions during our sexual intimacy.

And I have come to realize that the fullness of our lovemaking is dependent upon the degree of intimacy in our total relationship.''

QUESTIONS FOR REFLECTION

REMEMBER, the answers are inside you. Writing in your notebook will help you discover them.

1. *Are we growing as a loving couple or are we living as "married singles?"*
2. *In what basic areas of our marriage do I feel disagreement and division?*
3. *At the present time, which are the signs or symptoms of spiritual divorce in our marriage relationship?*
4. *Which of those symptoms do I feel responsible for?*
5. *What are the consequences of spiritual divorce in our personal lives, in our marriage, and in our family life?*
6. *Are there causes of those symptoms in my personal life?*
7. *What am I doing to overcome the causes of spiritual divorce in our relationship?*
8. *What could or should I do?*
9. *What could or should we do together?*
10. *How can we improve our conjugal communication and dialogue?*
11. *Do we need some kind of professional help or advice? What kind?*
12. *Do we need to deepen our relationship with God? How?*

The
Third Day

FACING MARRIAGE REALITY

Unhappiness in marriage is caused mainly by the failure of the couple to cope with the difficult parts of a marriage relationship, namely, crises, conflicts and problems.

Basically, marriage is a loving relationship between a man and a woman. Traditionally, married couples were challenged to stay together:

> "For better or for worse
> For richer or for poorer
> In sickness and in health
> Until death do you part."

At the same time, there was a tendency to emphasize parent-hood almost exclusively. But times have changed. There is an urgent need to stress the marital relationship in order to prevent couples from the destructive potential of contemporary megatrends, like individualism, materialism, hedonism, consumerism, and secularism.

To become a happy couple today, you have to face the challenges of marriage courageously by dealing with crises, conflicts and problems together.

CRISES

The word "crisis" sounds like a dirty word in most marriages. It carries the connotation of fighting, arguments, strife and troubles. However, crisis is a fact of married life. Instead of being seen as a potential death of the marriage, it can be viewed as an opportunity to grow. Crisis is a sign of life. And, a marriage without crisis belongs in a cemetery!

If a couple is afraid to confront crises in their marriage, they usually wind up running away from their reality or denying reality exists. When married couples can no longer avoid crises, they find they are unable to communicate and therein begins the deterioration of their relationship. Unless and until a couple is committed to face crises in their marriage together, they will be unable to become a happily married couple.

The American Institute of Family Relations gives four warning signals of a troubled marriage that should never be ignored, even if the spouses are sure they have a "good marriage."

1. The bottling up of feelings and resentments by either party.
2. A lack of agreement about family decisions.
3. Problems with or about their sexual relationship.
4. Signs of depression or withdrawal by one of the partners.

CONFLICTS

Actually, the failure to overcome a crisis is almost always because of the inability of husband and wife to deal creatively with their conflicts. Conflict is a signal that there is something in a marriage relationship that needs attention from both spouses. Conflicts may be unpleasant, but when handled properly they are a potential for growth and an opportunity to achieve greater intimacy. Conflicts can be just disagreements heated up by anger. So to handle conflicts properly we must deal with anger constructively.

Anger is a strong feeling, but as a feeling it is not wrong or bad. It shouldn't be denied or bottled up. It should be expressed creatively. And, until spouses can share and manage their anger towards each other they will never have an intimate relationship.

How to manage anger in your marriage?

1. It is necessary to discover the root of your anger, i.e., your hurts, misunderstandings, disappointments, fears, frustrations, dissat-

isfactions, needs, tensions, stresses, illnesses, and injustices. In other words, deal with angry situations and settle the issue that lies behind your anger. You have to find out what is causing it. If you don't, the issue will still be present and can surface at any time in the future.

2. Use your anger **constructively** by realizing and recognizing that you are angry. Let your spouse know it as soon as possible through an honest and lively dialogue. In that way, you both will be able to understand what you can do about it together.

3. You can make some kind of written and signed commitment about how to handle your anger, like: "When angry, I will acknowledge my anger and tell **you** I am angry at the first opportunity."

PROBLEMS

Problems in married life are unavoidable. They are a challenge for deepening your relationship and consequently, a unique opportunity for becoming a happier married couple. All you need is the firm and profound conviction that there is no problem in your life that you cannot solve together. Try it and you will experience amazing revelations.

How should you handle your marital problems? I would suggest three steps:

First, reflect individually and answer in writing these four questions:
1. What is the problem?
2. What are the internal, and what are the external causes?
3. What can I do personally to solve it?
4. What kind of help and cooperation do I need from you?

Second, separately, write a "love letter" to your spouse, sharing with him/her what you have reflected on and written about for the four previous questions.

Third, come together to:
1. Exchange your "love letters."
2. Afterwards, have some loving comments to emphasize your positive and common grounds. Make a commitment toward a loving action.

What can you do if your partner isn't cooperative?
I would suggest:

1. You take the first step by having an honest and deep personal reflection to discover in yourself the possible roots of your partner's unwillingness to work on your relationship.

2. Write a "love letter" to your spouse — confessing your own faults and deficiencies, evaluating, recognizing and praising each one of his/her efforts, and asking for forgiveness and help.

3. At the most opportune time, generously offer as a gift your "love letter," without asking anything in return.

TESTIMONIES

"Right now we are not in a crisis in our marriage, though we have had some in the past. However, conflicts and problems which test our covenant and offer an opportunity to grow closer to each other and to deepen our commitment to each other and God, do come up with regularity in our life.

This step was helpful to us for focusing in on what our present experience is of our relationship; what areas of conflict we have now and how we are working on our relationship. This was important because there is a tendency to fall back onto old statements about the way we were rather than to be totally honest and courageous about what is happening right now. This allowed us to focus on the last few weeks and to be more candid about what really is happening to us."

"For the past few years, Mike and I suffered terribly because of a problem I was having. I had begun to drink heavily, and I was not able to control it. I knew there was something terribly wrong but I hid it from everyone including Mike, because I was fearful, guilty, and felt that I could not live without alcohol.

Mike sensed that there was something seriously wrong, and tried to help, but was not aware of what was causing the change in me. Finally, after much prayer and suffering, I was given the grace to face my problem, admit it to myself and others, and I am now a member of Alcoholics Anonymous. I also see an Alcoholic Counselor once a week. Physically I am in pretty good shape. Emotionally and spiritually I am struggling to get better.

30

Our marital communication has been growing and deepening during these past months. Our relationship is better now, after several years of dishonesty. At this point in my life, I am trying to be extremely watchful of emotions such as anger and resentment. Through the A.A. program, I am learning how to handle these emotions and finding out that an alcoholic cannot afford the "luxury" of these emotions.

I am changing each day and working very hard on my attitudes and feelings, and discovering that I can live a very full, rich life without the crutch of alcohol. I thank God for Mike who stood by me and loved me through it all."

QUESTIONS FOR REFLECTION

How many of the following questions are you ready to respond to in your notebook?

1. *Could I describe our present relationship with just a few words?*
2. *Do I feel satisfied with the level of intimacy and mutual openness we have in our marriage?*
3. *Which are the major differences or disagreements between us?*
4. *When was the last time the two of us did something enjoyable alone together? What did we do?*
5. *At the present time, do we have any crisis in our marriage?*
6. *What do I usually do when I feel angry?*
7. *What is the most important problem in our present married life?*
8. *What are the roots of that problem in me?*
9. *Am I jealous, selfish, arrogant or uncooperative?*
10. *Could we increase our intimacy and mutual openness?*
11. *What should I do personally to improve our relationship?*
12. *What could I do to intensify our togetherness?*

DISCOVERING MARRIAGE POTENTIAL

In your effort to become aware of "Where Are We?"
As a married couple
You have to realize
The whole reality of your marriage.

Previously,
You dealt with the painful part
Of your marriage relationship:
Spiritual divorce,
Crises,
Conflicts and Problems.

Now,
You are invited to experience
a marvelous discovery:
The potential you have
as a married couple —
Your conjugal values.

VALUES

What are values? They are defined as "those qualities we hold dear." I would describe them as — those powerful **energies** hidden within us waiting to be released to become the **moving** force of our life. Values are the positive side of our reality, even in times of evolution and change.

Most people ignore their values or have no awareness of their potential. Nonetheless, values are real. They are at the center of our being, shaping our ideals, influencing our behavior and keeping us moving in life.

We have values as individuals, as couples, as families and as communities. Here, we are dealing with the values you have as a married couple.

MARRIAGE VALUES

Married people are generally unaware of the tremendous potential they have because of their common values as a couple. They ignore them, and consequently feel empty and unhappy in their marriage. The discovery of marriage values is very important, not just for the couple and their children, but for society too. Of course, to identify marriage values is not an easy task. It is hard to believe people who at times are petty, self-centered and irritable, can actually make each other happy. But it is possible.

After many years of ministering to and with married couples, I have come to a hopeful conclusion. Within each and every married couple there is a hidden treasure of divine energy of love, waiting to be discovered and released. To encourage you in this exciting discovery of your hidden treasure, I will concentrate on three major values: Marriage Life, Marital Sexuality, Conjugal Love.

MARRIAGE LIFE

The potential of **living together,** as husband and wife, through a growing and loving relationship, is what marriage is all about. But journeying-together in life is not always easy, as you know. Togetherness implies a willingness to accept one another's differences and deficiencies; to get along without surrendering the individuality of either; to help and support each other's weaknesses; to share and enrich one another with their personal strengths and sacrifices. That is why life, when viewed as a journey of life-together, is never complete. There is always another step to take, another dimension to

33

discover, another challenge to face, or another call to answer.

The marriage of a couple who stops walking-together in life, will die. This is the tragic experience of millions of today's married couples. Therefore if you want your living-together to be a success, you both have to go through the Four Seasons of Marriage:

The Spring of Love: This is the "romantic" time of longing for each other; it is a time to look in each other's eyes, and enjoy every moment together.

The Winter of Togetherness: This is the "painful time" of realizing differences; experiencing frustration, misunderstanding, doubt, confusion, jealousy, hate, indifference and loneliness. This is the opportunity for recognizing mistakes and faults, and suffering and maturing together. It is a time for mutual reconciliation.

The Summer of Relationship: This is the "peaceful time" of enjoying intimate, deep and loving person-to-person-relationship. It is the dialogue time.

The Autumn of Marriage Life: This is the "faithful and hopeful time" of going-beyond-you-and-me. It is a time for "trialogue" or praying-together.

If you cope with each of these times, alone and together, you will win a very special marathon — the Marathon of Marriage Life.

MARITAL SEXUALITY

The potential of marriage sexuality's fulfillment is another value husband and wife can develop together.

How?

First of all, by not confusing sexuality with biological or genital sex. Of course, biological sex is a part of human sexuality, but it is much more than that.

Second, by differentiating between sexuality and love. Indeed, human sexuality cannot be correctly understood apart from its intrinsic involvement with love.

Third, by being aware that sexuality is not a substitute for true happiness or for God. Ours is a sex-obsessed society where millions of men and women of all ages are bitterly realizing that sex, although it is a wonderful part of our nature, is not the meaning of our lives nor the fulfillment of our dreams.

Fourth, by developing the spiritual dimension of marriage sexuality through a serious exchange with the spouse of one's whole life, by becoming "one flesh."

Sexuality is a precious seed that is given you for furthering and strengthening your marriage and family life.

CONJUGAL LOVE

The potential of conjugal love is the essence of married life. It is also the only healthy way to survive, to grow, and to become a happy couple. When a husband and wife stop loving each other, their marriage gets sick and dies.

Why?

Because true love is the core and the soul of genuine marriage. True love includes: free decision, unconditional acceptance, unselfish affection and life-time dedication and service. When this is mutual, you will have a loving relationship; you will be fulfilled as a person, as a couple and as a family.

Love is, after all, the reason most often given for getting married. Loss of love is the reason most often given for dissolving a marriage. Love's capacity depends on the ability to find ways and means of expressing it. Love is not an idea or a feeling word. Loving is an action word.

Personal honesty, truthfulness, fidelity, humility, respect, understanding, acceptance, forgiveness, communication, mutual trust and confidence, mutual help, support and openness, are some of the key traits of conjugal love. In fact, married love is the most complex and complete expression of human love. And, most married people have a greater capacity for loving than they ever attempt to use.

TESTIMONIES

WHAT DO I VALUE MOST IN OUR MARRIAGE?

- "Looking for the values in our marriage has been very useful to us. If we were to inherit a box of gems we would look at them from time to time. So it is with our marriage values.
- "We like to reflect about our values. Every time we do, we feel encouraged that the two of us have such a clear gift of mutual confidence and unity. Then we feel more motivated to love one another through this precious gift."
- "We value our mutual love, our sexual intimacy and our children, but most of all, our faith in God and our respect for God's will in our lives."
- "Our ability to resolve conflicts and problems in constructive ways is one of our precious values."

- "Our friendship is very dear to us. We are each other's best friend. It is nice to love and to be loved this way."
- "Our mutual trust and confidence. We have no room for hatred, envy, jealousy, selfishness or conceit in our marriage. We only have room for leniency, good-heartedness, generosity and acceptance."
- "We are usually in agreement about where we are going and how we plan to get there. This is something we appreciate most in our relationship."
- "Our partnership. We feel and behave as equals."
- "Our sexual relationship, expression of our love, caring, sharing, touching and true fidelity. Our relationship is mirrored in our sexual fulfillment by working on our total relationship."
- "Our communication, togetherness and our relationship with God as individuals and as a couple."

QUESTIONS FOR REFLECTION

The following questions can help you to release the tremendous energy of love within you.

1. *Are we aware of our marriage potential?*
   Positive and negative signs of my awareness.
2. *Which are the most important values in our marriage?*
3. *Am I aware of the precious value of living together?*
   Positive and negative signs in my life.
4. *Do we have sexual and emotional harmony?*
   Why "yes," or why "no?"
5. *Are our sexual relations an expression of my true love?*
6. *Have we freely decided to be for one another in our marriage?*
7. *Do we mutually accept each other as we are?*
8. *Do we show interest in our mutual affection?*
9. *Are we at each other's service and dedicated to each other?*
10. *Is there any tension between us regarding life, sex and love? How can we overcome these tensions?*
11. *With reference to the three major values, which one needs to be developed most by us? Why? How?*
12. *Are there any anti-values in our marriage for which I feel strongly responsible? Which ones?*

IDENTIFYING MARRIAGE NEEDS

In order to face
Your total marriage reality honestly,
You have to deal with
Not just your marriage potential and values,
But you also have to realize
Your marriage needs.

The purpose of this day is
To guide you
In identifying your needs
As a married couple.
From there, you will evaluate
The manner in which you
Actually are responding
To those common needs:
In your journey
To become
A healthy and happy
Married couple.

THE BASIC NEEDS OF MARRIED COUPLES

From my personal experience in my years of full time ministry to, and with, married couples, I have learned there are five primary human needs of every married couple: Intimacy, Communication, Unity, Openness and Spirituality.

Let us concentrate on each one of these five important marriage needs.

INTIMACY

Intimacy is a natural fruit of a mature relationship. Therefore, it is strongly needed in every marriage.

After years of sharing the same house, the same table and the same bed, you may yearn for more closeness with each other. Sometimes, while you yearn for closeness, you also fear it, perhaps more than you fear anything else. You may be afraid to lose your personal individuality, or afraid your partner will discover your flaws and weaknesses, and reject you. You may remember the hurt you suffered before, when you allowed yourselves to be close to each other. And you are determined never to risk it again. Because of this, you learn and use all kinds of tricks to avoid getting close, even though you yearn for it and need it.

Partners are not always alike in their desire or tolerance for intimacy. Yet, if you overcome your fear of it, you will discover that both of you want the same intimacy in your special relationship.

There are many different levels of intimacy: emotional, social, intellectual, recreational, spiritual, physical and sexual. If you want to increase the level of your intimacy, you need to reveal more about your thinking, your feelings, your desires and your dreams.

The degree of your intimacy is in proportion to the amount of mutual trust, confidence and self-revelation in your relationship.

COMMUNICATION

Without communication between husband and wife, it is impossible to become a happily married couple. Interpersonal communication, i.e., person -to-person-communication, is the practical and concrete way to grow and mature in love, by giving to, and receiving from, each other.

How can this basic need be satisfied?

As mentioned before, the only way is by sharing with each other **your innermost self** — not just thoughts, judgments and feelings. But for this communication to be effective, you will need quality time together. Otherwise, your desire for communication will be just an unfulfilled dream and a yearned for utopia.

The number one enemy of marriage communication is individualism — a selfish tendency to be, move and act just as an independent single individual, without taking your partner into consideration.

UNITY

The eagerness to become one is the real meaning of the nature of married life. It is the highest dream of every sincere and genuine married couple. But unity is not uniformity. Unity encompasses differences and variety. Uniformity doesn't. Unity is not a simple feeling of closeness. It goes beyond that. Unity is a gift, given to those who honestly walk together in the same direction and with the same loving purpose in life.

How do you respond to this precious need in a creative way?

Mainly, by accepting your mutual differences, sharing your personal values, searching for those things which unite you instead of what separates you. In this way you become "one flesh."

Pride is the strongest enemy of true unity. It is a vicious tendency to give with arrogance and never be able to receive anything from anyone. The other enemy is selfishness, a tendency to receive but not give.

OPENNESS

Unity without openness is a false unity. It is a trap, a vicious circle of "just the two of us." Openness in marriage is a need, a need to go beyond "you and me," to become a living spiral, always open to life and to love.

How do you do it? Basically by:

a. Becoming aware of your common mission in life as a married couple.
b. Making a serious commitment to accomplish this mission.

39

c. Taking care of the needs of your children first and, afterwards,

d. Reaching out to the needs of others around you.

SPIRITUALITY

In today's materialistic society, most people do not care about the spiritual element. We are so concerned and involved with material things, we lose the true meaning of human life — spirituality. In fact, many contemporary marriages die for lack of spirituality.

Why?

Because marriage without spirituality is like a body without life. This is what marriage spirituality is all about: its life, its spirit, its soul, its deep meaning, its creativity, its transcendental dimension, its sacredness, and its mystery. In one word, its reference to God, the Creator. Therefore, spirituality is the most radical need in marriage. Without it, it will be unlikely that the other needs of a married couple will be fulfilled.

TESTIMONIES

LOVE

"I believe our love is even more basic than our sex life. Our sex life is fabulous and growing. But if our spirits, minds, emotions and wills — as well as our bodies — weren't in tune with God and each other, our good sex wouldn't last."

"Our friendship is fostered by the time we spend with each other and the things, including the many fun things, we do together. Being thoughtful and concerned about each other, which I believe we usually are, also helps."

UNITY

"We seem to be coping very well with our needs. It is becoming so natural to complement each other rather than compete. I feel very grateful for what we have with each other rather than dwelling on what we don't have.

COMMUNICATION

"The most important need in our marriage is communication. We need to share together each other's hurts and joys. We are coping with that need by trying to become more loving and understanding of each other."

"We need to learn to communicate without becoming so defensive. It causes so many arguments. We need to have a more loving attitude, to encourage and compliment each other, and we need to laugh more. We need to be aware of the good qualities we have and not be so hard and critical of ourselves."

OPENNESS

"We need to share our struggle with others. When we encourage our children or our friends, we feel the Lord's Joy because God is using us in this way."

"Openness is good but I don't feel heavily involved or committed with our ministry at this time. I believe God wants me/us to grow as a family. We need to be open to God's Grace to do it."

SPIRITUALITY

"Whether we admit it or not, our most important and basic need is our relationship with God, but I understand that if we don't have enough food and a place to live, it would be hard to concentrate on this. We need to pray more and to pray better together."

QUESTIONS FOR REFLECTION

CAUTION: The questions below relate to your needs as a couple. Next week you will deal with your individual needs.

1. *What are our basic needs as a married couple?*
2. *How are we fulfilling those needs?*
3. *What is our most important marriage need?*
4. *How am I responding to our most important needs?*
5. *What is our most urgent need?*
6. *Are we fulfilling it?*
7. *What kind of intimacy do we have?*
8. *Could we increase our marital intimacy? How?*
9. *Do we have deep communication? (Please clarify.)*
10. *Are there signs of unity in our married life? What ones?*
11. *Are we open and reaching out as a couple? (Please clarify.)*
12. *Do we take care of our spirituality as a married couple? How?*

The
Sixth Day

DISCERNING CONJUGAL LOVE

Marriage should be
A very special relationship
Between husband and wife.

If you want to find the key
For a happy marriage,
You have to deal very honestly
With the real meaning and human quality of your love.

But discerning love
Is not an easy task.
Love is difficult to understand
And even more difficult to put into practice.

Therefore,
You have to dedicate special time
To reflect and to share
About your conjugal love

This is precisely
The purpose of this sixth day.

THE REAL MEANING OF LOVE

Love is one of the more overused and misunderstood words. It's essence is sometimes completely distorted because of different interpretations.

One of the most common distortions is the contemporary tendency to identify love exclusively with sex. While it is true that sexual intercourse is a very vital and important aspect of conjugal love, it is only one expression of it. It is not its substitute. Another misinterpretation of the real nature of love is the tendency to confuse love with romantic sensations, emotions and feelings. Romantic feelings obviously play a big part in the relationship between husband and wife. It is also true that a healthy spirit of romance needs to be kept alive through a marriage, if it is to retain its spark. However, as love grows and develops, something deeper than romantic feelings is needed. You cannot base your conjugal love on the shifting sands of feelings, emotions and sensations.

To love is to accept the other as a person and as a whole. Of course, this free decision to accept the other is accompanied by feelings, emotions and sensations. These, however, are secondary to the priority of the decision and to the unconditional acceptance of the spouse.

LEVELS OF LOVE

To discern the real meaning and quality of your married love, you have to pay close attention to the different levels of love. Love develops and grows as the relationship changes and grows. To discern the meaning and quality of your conjugal love, you have to evaluate your personal intentions, purposes and attitudes in relationship with your spouse.

Level 1: Loving Yourself For The Sake Of Yourself.
Fair and just love of "self" — unconditional self-acceptance is the key for all kinds of love. Without it, you can't love your spouse.

Level 2: Loving Your Spouse For The Sake Of Yourself.
This is the love based on the old golden rule: "Love Your Neighbor As You Love Yourself." As a matter of fact, your spouse is your closest neighbor. This could be termed "Love of Friendship." It means a free decision, sincere acceptance and reciprocity.

Level 3: Loving Your Spouse For Your Spouse's Sake.
This is the unselfish and unconditional love. Its rule could be "Love Your Spouse As You Would Like To Be Loved."

Level 4: Loving Your Spouse For God's Sake.
This is Charity. Loving the spouse more than oneself. Being ready to die for him/her, with the Grace of God.

WAYS OF GROWING IN LOVE

Love isn't just something you feel; love is something you do. Couples who keep their love alive and growing are the ones who really work at their marriage. Marriage can be viewed as a fire.

To keep a fire burning brightly, there is one easy way: keep the two logs together, near enough to keep each other warm and far enough apart for breathing room.

Growing together is what love is all about. But as you can realize, growing relationships don't just happen; they are made day-by-day.

What can you do to rekindle the fire of love?

1. PRACTICE DAILY SIGNS OF LOVE
    Love's signs are a revelation of the energy of love that lies within you. They are a living testimony of your true love. They are sacramental: symbols of something beyond yourself. You will initiate them from the bottom of your heart. In the Appendix of this book, you will find some suggested signs of love to inspire you. Use your creativity for other signs.

2. EXPRESS APPRECIATION AND GRATITUDE
    Do not take each other for granted. Nurture your spouse's self-esteem by emphasizing his/her talents. Accept your spouse's appreciation of you. Look for opportunities to praise your mate in public, especially in front of your children, relatives and friends. Express your negative feelings without belittling your partner. Remember negative judgments make people feel unloved. Criticize sparingly. Say "thank you" for every loving gesture. Maintain a good sense of humor.

3. IMPROVE COMMUNICATION
    Love is . . . good communication. The single most important thing that will make you grow in love is communication. So keep lines of your interpersonal communication open 24 hours a day. If you have love, you will be actively searching for better communication with each other through:
    — Stressing the things which unite you rather than those which divide you.

44

— Sharing and bringing to each other your daily living experiences with trust and mutual confidence, as friends do.
— Asking for and offering forgiveness as soon as you are aware of your mistake, hurt or regret.
— Doing things together, like traveling, working on a project, dining, dancing and partying, sharing with your children, preparing home celebrations, vacationing together, praying etc.

TESTIMONIES

• Dear Ann!

"I find it difficult to write a love letter to you when we are struggling to find an answer to our sex problem. I love you deeply and yearn to feel even more unity in our marriage. We have come a long way.

I want to share everything with you. Sometimes I hold back because I am afraid that you will cry or be hurt. I have to be willing to risk, to trust in your goodness.

I have to listen very closely to you without judging or being critical.

I hope to set new goals for our marriage and move on to a more loving way.

I really don't want to live with anyone else. You are my life and my hope."

Love, Jerry.

• Dear Jerry!

"I want to take this time to tell you how much I love you and thank you for all you do for me.

I love the way you do special things for me. I'm sorry for the way I am, sometimes, with our sex life when I am not in the mood for sex. I find it very hard to let you know my true feelings about it.

I have to share my whole self with you.

We need more quality time together to share from within.

It is important that our time together not be interrupted. Our sharing can be so much deeper if we can continue to love. Beginning with a kiss helps to dissolve any tension that may be between us.

I would like also to have a better understanding of the Bible and what it means to us as a couple.

Please keep on being the caring and loving person that you are."

I love you, Ann

QUESTIONS FOR REFLECTION

This can be a barometer for realizing the present state of your married love if you reflect and write in your notebook about the following questions:

1. *What does love mean to me?*
2. *What kind of love is there in our marriage?*
3. *Do I love myself fairly and justly?*
4. *Do I accept my spouse as he/she is?*
5. *Do I treat my spouse the way I would like my spouse to treat me?*
6. *Do I listen to my spouse with my heart?*
7. *Am I aware of my spouse's needs?*
8. *Is my spouse aware of my personal needs?*
9. *Do I trust him/her?*
10. *Do I love my spouse for the sake of God?*
11. *What kind of love signs do I think my spouse needs from me?*
12. *How could we improve our conjugal love?*

FINDING QUALITY TIME TOGETHER

Sitting down and talking was easy before you were married.

It seemed so natural. You had a whole life to share.

Your journey had been on different roads. You could share your dreams, your hopes, everything.

Those moments were precious and very special for you.

But now, after all the years of marriage, it is not easy to sit down and talk any more.

Actually, when was the **last time** you spent together, to share from within?

The fact is, the lack of person-to-person communication between husband and wife is at the bottom of almost all marriage crises and problems, and consequently, a deep root of unhappiness in marriage.

Is this your personal experience?

I firmly believe that what married couples need and deserve to become a happily married couple, are not sophisticated theories and rhetorics about communication and dialogue.

Rather, they need real opportunities to experience an intimate, profound, intense and loving encounter between themselves, without any kind of interference or mediation.

It was precisely this personal conviction that encouraged me to originate and promote Marriage Encounter twenty-five years ago.

CONJUGAL DIALOGUE

There are hundreds of ways to be in touch with each other in marriage, but the number one way is dialogue.

What is conjugal dialogue?

It is a loving conversation between husband and wife with only one main purpose: listening to each other. Listening is the key word for creative dialogue. Without true listening there can be no dialogue, only discussion. Listening is to your dialogue what love is to your marriage.

But the question is how to truly listen to each other. The Chinese pictograph for "listen" is meaningful and inspiring. The character they use to express the verb "listen" is a combination of the root symbols used to describe the ears, minds, endurance, eyes, heart, and precious stone.

Namely:

Listening with your ears, to hear each word as something very special.

Listening with your mind, to humbly search for understanding.

Listening with your eyes, to consciously receive the non-verbal message.

Listening with your heart, to accept all with real love.

In this way, you enable your hearing, understanding, receiving and loving to be lasting and enduring, as a precious stone.

This is the kind of listening everyone longs for. When this listening is mutual, you are practicing creative conjugal dialogue.

MAKING QUALITY TIME TOGETHER

Time is the necessary ingredient for a creative dialogue. If you want to sincerely practice dialogue, you have to set aside quality time.

What is quality time?

It is your special time together. It is time not to criticize or blame each other, nor to solve problems or make demands. It is time to just listen to each other, from the bottom of your heart. It is time to be in touch with each other: alone, without interruptions, and without being rushed. Just the two of you in a special location.

The place is important to quality time. Find a place where you have privacy, can relax, feel rested and be alert. A place where you can look in each other's eyes, sit close, hold hands and have a pleasant and uplifting experience.

This time together has to be a high priority for the two of you, if you honestly want to find it, you will enjoy it. "I/We don't have time!" is an easy mask which hides something deeper. You know yourself well enough to admit that if something is important to you, you will find time for it. Besides, we all use 24 hours a day. The question is how you spend that time and what amount of that time is spent with your spouse.

According to my experience in marriage ministry, I would suggest having a dialogue time periodically — daily, weekly or monthly, depending on your particular needs, desires and mutual agreement. But always make it quality time — the best time for both of you. For instance, some couples for the daily dialogue have their short sharing time early in the morning, before their day begins. Others prefer the evening. Some like to dialogue during a shared meal or during a walk together. Others, at prayer time.

Each couple has to find their special time together according to their needs and circumstances. But find it! Otherwise you will not grow as individuals, nor as a happy couple.

Think about the time you spend together. Could it be put to better use? How? When?

Why not TODAY?

"A TIME FOR US"

If you both, individually, have finished reading, reflecting and writing in your notebook on the Questions for Reflection of the previous six days, find some quiet place in your home or away, where both of you can feel comfortable and alone, so you don't have to worry about being interrupted or overheard while you share.

HOW should your time be spent?

1. START with a short prayer, a song, or just a hug, a kiss, a caress.

2. EXCHANGE your notebooks.

3. READ with your heart, as well as with your head, your spouse's answers to the Questions for Reflection of the six previous days.

4. SHARE with each other about what touched you the most. Please, no arguing, quarreling, judging, problem-solving, or decision-making.

5. GIVE each other sincere and loving thanks for something specific and concrete.

6. THANK GOD together, if you both want to do it spontaneously.

7. ENCOURAGE each other to start and complete the Second Week, with renewed enthusiasm and hope.

8. CELEBRATE the finish of your first week in the manner you desire.

Who
Am
I?

Second Week

WHO AM I?

"The Purpose of Life Is To Be That Self Which One Truly Is"
Soren Kierkegaard

52

"Mirror, Mirror,
Who Am I?"

"Who Am I?" is the most profound question that you must deal with if you want to be honest with yourself and become fully human. In this second week, you are invited to experience a voyage toward the deepest and highest part of yourself.

"Who Am I?" is a challenging question for all of us. Generally we are afraid to face our self because we are guilty of not being who we really are. It is so much easier to escape and accept yourself as what you have let yourself become, than to go back and find the real you. It seems that we allow ourselves to learn about almost everything but our inner self.

This is the paradox of our times: while a few men and women are being launched into space to discover new worlds, many human beings die daily without discovering who they are. Our de-personalized society not only makes the process of identifying one's self difficult, but practically impossible.

Therefore, let us have the courage to confront this alienation and try to experience a deep and honest encounter with yourself.

Remember: unless you encounter your real self, you will be unable to encounter your spouse or anyone else.

You can do it!

If you do not do it, nobody else will do it for you.

The
First Day

BECOMING ONESELF

DISCOVERING YOUR INNER SELF

Cervantes, the Spanish writer, gives us wise advice: "Love not what you are, but only what you may become."

Inside each one of us, there is an inner self which strives for recognition and realization. "Self" is a mysterious word waiting to be discovered. Even though you are married, you are two different persons, each one unique unto yourselves.

In a system of priorities, the individual is first and the marriage, second. While we are similar in many ways as human beings, each of us is different as individuals. So never imitate. Do not try to be someone else. Just be yourself by respecting your full potential and your inner resources. The uniqueness of each person adds variety and richness to a relationship.

Many people today are searching for new dimensions to add to their daily lives. In other words, they are trying to realize their true, special, inner self. All too often, individuals seek to find, in another person, what exists only within the uniqueness of their self. No one will truly find his/her inner self by relying heavily upon the insights, evaluation and love offered by others. Your values come from within your real self. They do not come from what others think of you, but from the healthy and balanced appreciation you have of your own intrinsic worth.

Thus, you have to begin with the recognition that there is an internal self-energy of love within you, waiting to be actualized. Only when you realize you must stand on your own feet — however shaky your balance may then be — you will find that inner peace which comes from the awareness of knowing that you are a person.

As you move from your potential to your deeds, from your possibilities to your realization, you are becoming yourself.

BECOMING A PERSON

What does it mean to be a person?

According to scholars, a person is a unique individual who meets a high standard of achievement and has a sense of selfhood to realize his/her potential as a human being. In other words, you have a name, but you are not just a name. You are **someone.** You are not just a body and a mind. You are a person. Furthermore, you are a unique person, not meant to be a copy of anyone.

According to the Bible — Genesis, chapters 1 & 2 — we are persons because "God created us in His image and likeness," and God is Someone. He is The Person. When Moses asked Him for his name, God answered: "I Am Who I Am." — Exodus 3:14.

Therefore, each of us is an absolutely unique creation of God. Our dignity and our personal identification are rooted in God. Consequently, our first and greatest responsibility is to become the beautiful person God created us to be. A person is not born complete, but contains an enormous potential: all that is necessary to become complete. But nothing in the world is more painful than to take that path which leads to our true self.

It is strange, isn't it, that while all of us have the potential that could lead us to a rich and satisfying life, few of us develop it as much as we'd like. There are many reasons for this: number one is fear.

There is a lot of fear in everyone and it is very deep. It can take hold of you in many different ways. You may be afraid of changing from the old self to the new self. This can be a complex process requiring real effort and endurance. You might be afraid of being true to yourself, being free, being responsible — being a person.

BEING HONEST WITH YOURSELF

What is the key to overcoming all your fears and becoming the unique person you can be and you desire to be? The answer is simple, but not easy: Be honest with yourself! Honesty with one's self is the starting attitude to becoming yourself.

How can you get this self-honesty and be true to yourself?

a. By listening carefully to the voice of your conscience and following it faithfully.
b. By being open-minded and open-hearted. Openness will permit you to be vulnerable to the truth.
c. By thinking positive and searching for the positive.
d. By never telling lies and speaking only the truth.

e. By spending daily time looking and listening to what's going on within you, facing and accepting the positive and negative.
f. Knowing yourself better so you will be able to understand, to accept and to love your true self.
g. By not blaming others for your own limitations.
h. By taking care of yourself as well and as often as you take care of others. The more you take care of yourself the less frustration and anger you will feel, and the more you will become true to yourself, and consequently, to your spouse.

When every spouse in the world is honest with his/herself, every couple in the world will feel happier. They will then be true to each other and their families.

TESTIMONIES

FRED: Earlier this year I was given a special assignment on a high-level panel. I had mixed feelings. On the one hand I felt honored and elated, but I also was concerned about what would be involved.

The job turned out to be quite a challenge. Most of the men on the panel were aggressive, articulate people who had strong opinions that they readily shared. I tend to be more reflective and could hardly get a word in. In group situations I usually am able to act as a facilitator. I can focus in on the issues and then steer the group toward the logical conclusion. In this group, though, I was unable or unwilling to do this. I felt frustrated, afraid and inadequate.

Fortunately I was able to recognize that I am more important than the job. I was able to forget it when I left the office. I needed the serenity of our home and my time with Helen to recharge my batteries. I ate lunch at my desk, and then went for a walk to get a break from the activity. I was also able to recognize that, in my quiet way, I was contributing more than I realized. Time was on my side and I needed to hang in there and be myself. To try to slug it out, would have been counterproductive.

HELEN: As a wife, I believe God gave me the power to create the atmosphere in our home, if I know I'm important enough to take care of me first. I am trying to know my needs and realize doing isn't being. It's tough for me to give into myself when there's trauma in our life. It's easier for me to lash out at Fred and blame him for my uneasiness. I grew up hearing that giving in to "me" was being selfish. But I know I can give more to others when I'm rested.

When Fred is under extra stress because of the job, I give into myself through the day to make sure I'm relaxed and have energy to

56

be there for him. I try to provide an especially good dinner. I put him before things. I take care of me so I can be there for him at the end of the day. What he needs the most is to arrive home to a relaxed, happy wife.

MARY: "I cannot fully be a lover for my husband and help him feel like a lovable person unless I first love myself. I had a hard time accepting this during this week. I've heard these concepts before, but this time I experienced them."

QUESTIONS FOR REFLECTION

1. *Who am I?*
   Could you describe yourself in a few words?
2. *Am I happy being the person I am, or would I like to be a different kind of person?*
   What kind of person would you like to become?
3. *What are the main difficulties I have in becoming myself.*
   The internal as well as the external difficulties.
4. *How can I overcome these difficulties?*
   Think in practical ways.
5. *Am I honest with myself?*
   Find positive or negative signs of self-honesty.
6. *Do I really take care of myself?*
   If not, what can you do to be more serious about taking care of yourself?
7. *Do I spend daily time to look and listen to what's going on within myself?*
   If not, are you going to try it? How?

KNOWING YOURSELF

Sometimes we complain that other people do not understand us. Perhaps this is true. But what is truer, and much more important for us, is that we do not understand ourselves. This is one of the deep roots of emptiness, dissatisfaction and unhappiness in our lives. To understand ourselves as we really are, we have to be in intimate touch with our inner self and listen to it very carefully.

Through the ages, man and woman have been admonished to know themselves. Self — one's individual person — has been described as the center of our being. It is important that we come to understand it as the essence of our lives.

On the other hand, you have to remember that each self is unique. In all the world there is no other self like you. Nobody has your smile. Nobody has your eyes, your nose, your hair, your hands, your voice. Nobody sees things just as you do. Through all of eternity no one will ever look, talk, think or act like you. You are special.

Actually, what are you like?

UNDERSTANDING YOURSELF

If you want to find your self-portrait and understand your special self, you have to deal with the three dimensions of your inner self. They are your temperament, your character and your personality.

Your temperament. This is your physical constitution in so far as it effects your manner of sensing, thinking, feeling and acting. As a result of that natural mechanism — according to psychologists — various types of temperaments appear, corresponding to the different and peculiar tendencies of each individual. There are four classifications of these types of temperaments: most of us are a combination of two or more.
— Sanguineous — fullness of vigor and activity.
— Nervous — excitability and emotional impulses.
— Limphatic — calm, indolence, and inconstancy.
— Bilious — irritability, anger and sharpness.

Your Character. This includes your particular qualities and outstanding traits, derived from your family upbringing and your social education. It distinguishes you from others.

Your Personality. This is you as you answer to or as you present yourself to others.

TAKING OFF YOUR MASKS

In your journey toward yourself, you need an undistorted vision of your "inner self." To achieve this, you have to identify and face your masks.

What are masks all about? They are:
— Anything that covers up those thoughts, feelings, attitudes and purposes that cause you to conceal your real self.
— Things you do or ways you act to protect yourself from fears — fear of rejection, fear of not being accepted for who you are, fear of being attacked or ridiculed, fear of appearing to be weak or less than perfect, fear of not living up to what others expect you to be.
— Actions and behaviors you put on in order to appear to be what you are not but you would like to be.
— Whatever hides the real you that you are striving to become and share with others.
— Personal images of yourself that you are trying to protect or project.

At times it is so much more comfortable to put on a mask than to admit the reality of what you are sensing, feeling, thinking or doing. But when you come to grips with the reality of your sensing, feeling, thinking or doing, it is usually a relief. Then a sense of peace and accomplishment takes over. As you share this with someone you become liberated.

All this could be compared to being an egg. When you are letting your mask dominate you, you are like an egg — just sitting there, just existing. Taking off the mask is like the duckling breaking through the shell as it hatches. It is hard to break through the shell and so takes a lot of hard work. And you have to keep chipping away until you are out. But breaking out of the shell, while difficult, is the first absolutely necessary step to fulfill your potential of completely becoming whom you should be, and whom you want to be.

We've all worn masks from the time we were very young. But finding them is not so easy because it means stepping outside ourselves to see ourselves as others see us. And it means admitting that we are not as completely open with others and as secure within ourselves as we would like to be. In order to know yourself, and understand who and what you really are, you have to discover your masks and the real person you are behind them. Your honesty is the key for this discovery.

BEING A REFLECTIVE PERSON

Why do so many people have a self-knowledge that is deficient or inadequate? Why are they so unaware of what they are really like? Why are you not the person you would like to be? The main reason is lack of personal reflection and intimacy with oneself.

To be a reflective and intimate person is to be in direct touch with your inner-self: your thoughts, feelings and basic assumptions about life; your attitudes, your needs, your values, your goals and your priorities. If you do not know these things about yourself, you are less free and cannot make healthy decisions. Then you become a shallow, dissatisfied and unhappy person.

It isn't who you are, it is who you think you are, that sets the boundaries of your accomplishments. Therefore, it is very important for you and for your relationship with your spouse, your children and your neighbors that you become a reflective and intimate person.

How do you do it?

Here are five suggestions:

1. TIME. Set a date for an appointment with yourself.
2. PLACE. Find a spot free of noise and interruptions. Be alone.
3. CONCENTRATION. Listen carefully and the right questions and the right answers will come from within you.
4. HONESTY. Be open with yourself. Listen sincerely. Don't cheat yourself.
5. WRITING. Express in writing what you are hearing from within you. It will be a self-revelation.

Take courage!

Your life is in your hands through your personal reflection. You can make it whatever you desire. You are free to build or to destroy, to be strong or weak, successful or unsuccessful, happy or miserable.

It's all a matter of channeling the personal energy within you that is waiting to be released.

TESTIMONIES

FRANK: "Behind my reflective nature is my 'good guy' mask. If I don't criticize them, hopefully they won't criticize me. My fragile ego and need to be perfect won't permit this. If I wait passively to see what the other person wants, and try to give it to him, maybe he will like me. By not being myself I am cheating us both. He isn't able to see the beautiful person I am. By trying to manipulate others it makes it difficult for them to show their unique beauty.

"Another aspect of my inability to deal with negative feelings toward other people is that I store up resentment and hostility. Recently at work there was a high level presentation to be given. There were two of us on the panel who could have done it. The other man, Bill, is smart, articulate and effective. Yet for several reasons it was appropriate for me to give the presentation.

"My passive, 'don't accept responsibility' tendency wanted me to let Bill do it. Yet I knew the tough but right thing was for me to do it. He readily agreed and sat down to help me prepare the charts.

"His style is so different from mine, and he comes on so strong, that I knew I had to do the first cut at the charts myself. I told him bluntly I wanted to do this. He felt hurt and a little rejected but something inside me told me this had to be. I got them done and asked for his review. We made minor changes and the presentation was very good.

"I wished I could have been more loving, but when you aren't used to being assertive, it's difficult. I felt grateful I was able to face what I wanted and ask for it in such a loving way. Years ago I would have gone along with him, felt hostile and resentful, and probably blown my stack at him. I felt thankful for the growth in me I could see.

"I reminded myself it doesn't matter how far I've come; what matters is that I'm on the right track."

KATHY: "I'm beginning to see how the answers are within me. This makes me realize my pattern of expecting others to take care of me. So much of my unhappiness is because of my 'poor me' attitude. I want my spouse to do for me what only I can do. But deep down I really don't know who I am. I'm excited, yet scared, to find out.

QUESTIONS FOR REFLECTION

1. *What are the three words that best describe me?*
   Just three words.
2. *Do I understand myself?*
   Write in your notebook what you like, and don't like, about yourself.
3. *What kind of temperament do I have?*
   You could be a combination of two or more.
4. *What are the outstanding traits of my character?*
   Think about your uniqueness or special qualities.
5. *Do I wear any "masks?" Which ones?*
   Try to describe one of them.
6. *Do I have a secret for living in peace with myself?*
   What is it?
7. *Am I a reflective person?*
   Write the positive and negative signs of self-intimacy in your present life.

The
Third Day

CLARIFYING YOUR PERSONAL VALUES

BECOMING AWARE OF YOUR PERSONAL VALUES

Psychologists agree that, hidden deep down inside ourselves, there is a multitude of mysterious forces and energies which affect our behavior. Our **values** are a portion of this powerful potential which we carry within ourselves and which influence our behavior.

Most people never seriously consider what their true values are, or even if they have any. But whether they discover them or not, values are at the bottom of every individual's being. They shape their ideas, feelings and attitudes, and affect their behavior.

Our lifestyle is largely based on our values, on what is important to us. Our values determine how we deal with such issues as social status, public image, use of money, sex, roles, morality, religion, social causes, politics, justice, sociability, choice of friends, parenting children, attitudes toward work or play, and the way we use leisure time. The clarifying process of your values can help you in making your daily decisions and choices.

Each day of your life you must make decisions. Some of them are minor, like, "Shall I read this or that book?" But some of them are major decisions, like, "Should I take that extra job to have more income or spend my extra time with my family?" "Should I get divorced or not?"

These are alternatives. Sometimes you have to decide among three or four choices while establishing priorities. Then the matter becomes increasingly difficult. A clear awareness of your personal values can be the key to reach your best choice and your right priority. The search for personal values is a lifelong quest that never ends.

Do you believe you know what your real values are?

EMPHASIZING YOUR MORAL VALUES

There are many kinds of values. Moral values, however, have always been the highest of all. This is especially so in today's materialistic society.

Moral values are always personal values. They can only be realized by men and women. People are the only ones to love and to hate, to be joyful and sorrowful. The importance of man's own being is far above what he does or doesn't do.

A person radiates moral values when he demonstrates simplicity, generosity, truthfulness, goodness, justice, honesty, peace, joy, prudence, courage, temperance and love.

Are these moral values given to you at birth? No! They can develop only through your conscious and free surrendering of yourself to these genuine values. As long as we blindly disregard moral values or choose to ignore the positive values inherent in truth, we cling to negative values of falsehood and injustice. We are incapable of moral goodness. As long as we are interested only in the question of whether something is "pleasing" or not, we cannot be morally good. Moral values are far more important than self-convenience and self-pleasantness.

It is only when you understand there are things in life which are "important of themselves," things that are beautiful, good, and true, will you ever realize moral values. These may be independent of your awareness of them. You must let yourself be formed by their law.

Only when you can see beyond your subject horizons — when you can stop saying, "What's in it for me?" will you know moral values. Only when you leave behind the narrowness of spirit and abandon yourself to that which is important in itself — the true, the good, the just, the beautiful — will you become the bearer of moral values.

A moral person is a reverent person. Reverence is the mother of all moral life. It opens our spiritual eyes and enables us to grasp values. The irreverent person is closed within him or herself. He or she is myopic, and blind to values. The world refuses to reveal its beauty to him or her. Reverence is the essential element of moral life and moral values. Revere yourself, and you will value all your world: your spouse, your children, your family and your community. By revering yourself you are replacing the junk with the goodness of you. You value yourself!

CLARIFYING YOUR PERSONAL VALUES

Your real values may not be what you think. Many people confuse their values with their ideals. Your ideals, which in fact do affect your personal life, can motivate you in your quest for your real values, but your ideals are not your values in themselves. They are just indicators of which values you have.

Other indicators are your top priorities — what you really consider most important in your personal life. The best way to clarify and determine what your real values are is to consider where you:

spend your time
spend your money
spend your energy
are willing to risk.

Real values are measured mainly by what you invest in those four key indicators. The ways you: spend your time, your money, your energy and are willing to risk, indicate your authentic values.

For example, you may think that your marriage is your highest priority until you realize that you are actually investing much more of yourself in terms of your time, money, energy and risks, in doing social or apostolic work, drinking or playing.

Do you want to clarify what your real values are? Read the Testimonies and answer the "Questions for Reflection" by writing in your notebook.

It could be a turning point in your life!

TESTIMONIES

MAX: "I work hardest and longest at my job on business trips. Some of the best work I do is on airplanes, preparing for meetings, writing up reports, etc. Often times I will spend several hours in the motel room in the evening working — something I would never do at home. It is like a quid pro quo. They do something for me — paying my expenses to go to a neat location. This boosts my self-esteem and I pay them back by giving 125% effort. At home I will spend 30 minutes or so talking to Linda when I get home from work, plus additional time with her in the evening. Our relationship and marriage come ahead of the job. But when I'm on a trip it's great to give extra to my employer.

"I expend a lot of energy planning trips for Linda and me. I feel excited and fulfilled at the thought of going some place we've never been before. And it gives me satisfaction to get a bargain. Right now I'm working to get us a cruise at half-price. I feel excited at the prospect, concerned the deal isn't genuine and we will lose our money, and annoyed at the lackadaisical attitude of the travel agent.

"I invest my money with greatest enthusiasm by supporting persons who help others in a very practical and efficient way. I feel fulfilled and needed by giving to them.

"I'm not one to risk, but years ago I put our savings in the stock market to make enough money to put our 5 sons through college. Their future and well being is very important to me. Incidentally, they made it through in spite of the money I lost in the stock market.

"What does this tell me about my values? I have a need to receive and desire to give. I value our marriage and our family. I like to do fun things with Linda and to save money when I do it."

LINDA: "Knowing my priorities of God first, Max, my family and then friends and things brings me inner peace and helps me with making decisions.

"Making sure my husband comes before my children makes me feel on the right track and comfortable. His needs before theirs; our relationship needs to come before others.

"When I tell ladies I don't want to play tennis on the weekend because I have more fun spending time with my husband, I feel grateful and thankful for my priorities.

QUESTIONS FOR REFLECTION

1. *What do I esteem most important in my life?*
   Think about your most precious treasure.
2. *Specifically, what are my moral values?*
   Just list them.
3. *On what do I invest my time with most interest?*
   Be honest!
4. *On what do I spend my money most generously?*
   How much?
5. *On what do I spend my energy with most enthusiasm?*
   Why?
6. *In what area do I take the greatest risk?*
   Do you feel good about it?
7. *Among my values, which are in danger of being lost?*
   Explain this possibility.

MEETING YOUR PERSONAL NEEDS

You are now halfway to the interior of your self. If you want to discover the roots of your behavior and actions — like "Why do I do this or that?" — you have to look at your personal needs.

The objective of this day is to help you identify your own real needs with the purpose of satisfying them appropriately and avoiding the easy and common temptation of meeting your needs with escapes, substitutes, or more specifically, with drugs or alcohol, as many people do today.

It is a fact that any time you don't get your needs met, you become frustrated. Once you know your needs, you can establish your priorities. This will help you think things through more clearly and in the proper perspective.

NEEDS

Needs do not require definition or description. Everyone knows, understands and feels what needs are all about. Daily, we relate to our needs when we eat, drink, breathe, work, sleep, talk, cry, laugh or pray. We know what a need is, but frequently we ignore what our real and urgent needs are. Consequently, we do not act according to our priorities and our total well-being. We also easily confuse wants and needs. One way to distinguish them is to see needs as being essential, while wants deal with frills.

KINDS OF NEEDS

According to psychologists, there are different levels of basic human needs:
— Physiological: breathing, eating, drinking, etc.
— Psychological: having privacy, having self-esteem, etc.
— Moral: being respected, accepted, appreciated, etc.
— Spiritual: finding truth, freedom, goodness, beauty, etc.
— Social: having relationships, communicating, sharing, etc.
— Religious: searching for God, believing, praying, etc.
Some of our needs, especially those related to our own body, are so basic they are obvious. Social needs are sometimes obvious and sometimes subtle. The most subtle needs are those which are related to our inner self. They come about from very deep personal experiences and feelings. Sometimes we are aware of these needs and sometimes we are not.

The need of loving and being loved is so fundamental that when this need is not met, human existence becomes meaningless, absurd and unbearable. Then pills and/or alcohol enter our lives.

FACING THE REALITY OF "DRUGS"

In looking at "drugs" — as a substitute for, or escape from, our innermost needs — we must realize there are many kinds of "drugs" which are offered to us daily. And they're offered in very cunning ways to meet all kinds of needs. Some are: food, overwork, too much television and movies, and the obsessive desire for romance and erotic pleasures.

But the "chemical drugs" are the most dangerous. These might be alcohol, pills such as tranquilizers or pain killers or muscle-relaxers.

As you know, there are millions of "drug addicts" in today's world. This is unfortunate because it has been shown scientifically that drug addiction destroys our personality at its deepest roots.

The next step is dysfunctional behavior. The final step, suicide.

According to scientists, the drug problem and the sociological escapes are a very complex phenomenon. People often turn to drugs because of their inability to understand themselves. When they do this, they are unable to establish healthy relationships with others. Then they attempt to satisfy their relationship needs with more drugs.

Needs used to be real, natural and normal. Today, though, in our materialistic society, there is an increasing and aggressive promotion of artificial needs, especially through mass media. The desire to have more and to do more is killing the desire to be and to become yourself.

Sociological data tells us that the problem of alcohol and drugs in marriage and family life is a complex social problem rooted in the inability of husband and wife to fulfill their basic and personal needs in a healthy and constructive way. Unless you identify and satisfy your natural and real needs, you can't understand other people's needs: your spouse's, your children's and others.

FULFILLING YOUR REAL NEEDS

Searching For a Supportive Relationship

Once you have been honest with yourself by recognizing your real needs — in order to avoid becoming addicted to any kind of drugs, or to stop using them — you have to reach the conviction that you need a person who supports you: someone who listens, understands, encourages, nurtures, protects and cares, especially when you feel vulnerable.

When you were a child you were aware of your need for nurturing and support. As you grew up you may have lost touch with some of your dependency needs. Yet you never outgrow your need for emotional and personal support.

This need for a supportive relationship is a primary underlying motive for marriage — though people are not always aware of the wisdom of the Biblical revelation: "It is not good for man to live alone. I will make a suitable companion to help him." Genesis 2:18.

When the needed emotional support is lacking, loneliness, dissatisfaction and frustration invade a marriage relationship.

Couples need to learn to respond to each other's everyday emotional needs on a daily basis. However, adequate nurturing and support become critical in such vulnerable situations as sickness, disappointment, anxiety or loss. Therefore, a supportive and nurturing relationship provides a secure base for meeting your deepest needs.

Asking For Support Not For Rescue

You have to help your spouse understand the kind of support you need. In most situations you may only need your partner to listen attentively and let you know he/she understands and cares.

Sometimes, you may need your partner to "hear" and respond to the feelings underneath your words. Other times, you may need your partner to touch or hold you in a supportive and caring way. What you usually need, however, is not for your spouse to advise — unless you request it.

Not Confusing Nurturing With Sexual Needs

Since nurturing and sex are both intimate, warm and physical, they are easily confused. In the confusion neither nurturing nor sexual needs are adequately satisfied or met. People get momentarily excited about sex but most of the time they yearn for a good listener, understanding, emotional support and unconditional love.

TESTIMONIES

STEVE: "I am becoming more aware of my needs and wants. I grew up trying to cater to and anticipate my mother's needs so she would take care of me. This necessitated my hiding from my own needs for fear they would conflict with mom's. I felt angry, frustrated and hostile toward my mother. But I remained passive and afraid to be assertive and open, for fear of losing my favored position. My greatest personal need at this time is in preparing for retirement. I want to learn to get satisfaction for myself from doing things that give me fulfillment for myself as a unique individual. It also involves learning how to relate to Doris."

DORIS: "Our sharing each evening does so much for my self worth. I need to feel more important than Steve's job, and having him there for me in a loving, supportive way makes my day worthwhile. I need to feel needed but I also need to know I'm loved and appreciated for who I am as well as what I do."

ROSIE: "I'm hurting so much because I'm looking outside myself for a joy that is inside me. I don't know what my personal needs are because it's been too scary to admit 'the buck stops here.' If

I am not happy with myself, I can't expect anybody else to be happy with who I am. Now I know my deepest need is to get to know me better. I need to love me more."

QUESTIONS FOR REFLECTION

1. *What are my real needs?*
   Reflect about your basic and deepest needs.
2. *In what area is my greatest personal need at this time?*
   Think about your work, marriage relationship, sex, etc.
3. *How am I responding to my needs in a constructive way?*
   Concentrate on the present.
4. *Am I addicted to any kind of "drugs?"*
   Which ones?
5. *What need do I have that I most want to be fulfilled?*
   Write about an emptiness inside you.
6. *Do I feel fulfilled in my need to love and be loved?*
   List the persons you love and feel loved by the most.
7. *What do I really need from my spouse in order to fulfill my deepest needs?*
   Be sincere, specific and loving.

The
Fifth Day

ACCEPTING YOURSELF

IMPROVING YOUR SELF-IMAGE

We often speak of an image in regard to a person studying self in a mirror. When you look at yourself in a mirror you are aware that you see an image. The image is you and yet not as you really are. Your image in the mirror displays only the external characteristics, not the internal or spiritual. Your self-image is what you think and feel you are, both externally and internally.

Whether you realize it or not, you carry within you a mental picture of the kind of person you think you are. The picture is real even though you cannot touch or see it. Its influence in your life is very real. Your self-image affects your feelings, actions, behaviors, even your abilities. Your abilities and your self-image always go hand in hand.

The image you have of yourself is shaped by your relationship with other people. It develops from the attitudes of others towards you. According to psychologists, these attitudes go way back to when you were a little child. Therefore, what you think others think about you forms your self-image. Also, your self-image develops from your lived experiences, your gifts, and your limitations.

Your self-image can be positive or negative. If you see yourself as someone who is O.K., a worthwhile person, independent of what you can do, you have a positive and healthy image. If you see yourself as not having such worth or as incapable of doing much, then you have a poor or negative self-image.

The mental picture you carry of yourself is a vital factor in determining the richness and quality of life and your relationships. If you have a poor or negative concept of yourself, you will be vulnerable in potentially intimate and long term relationships. If you picture yourself as having little value you will feel unlovable and, therefore, will expect rejection. The pain of being rejected will stymie the closeness and intimacy of your relationships.

72

Your attitude towards others tells a lot about how you think and feel about yourself.

How you see yourself will influence how you live, also. A poor self-image is one of the main causes of disorientation, confusion and depression. By trying to please others so you can feel worthy and appreciated by them, you become guided, not by your real needs and your own wants, but by what others want and desire.

A positive self-image is an essential element in the process of self-identity. It is imperative for a meaningful and fulfilling marriage.

DEEPENING YOUR SELF-ESTEEM

Self-esteem is a positive, fair and healthy love of self. It is a quiet sense of self-respect and self-confidence, a thoughtful feeling of self-worth. Self-esteem means, for the most part, to feel good about yourself, to feel lovable. Self-esteem is not constant — we all have periods of depression, ups and downs, hard luck and bad times, but it comes through even when you meet with discouragement, failure or frustration. Your love for yourself is genuine, mature and healthy when you see yourself in truth, as you actually are.

The unhealthy love of self is selfishness: the attitude that includes an undue regard for self. The love of self is unhealthy and immature when self is accented in excess. When fairness and balance are missing, the attitude of selfishness takes place. This is precisely what happens when we focus our attention on what we have and do instead on focusing our attention upon who we really are. A healthy love for oneself must not be confused with selfishness and narcissism. Self-inflation and aggrandizement is a subtle mask for self-contempt and self-hatred.

Positive self-esteem is our deepest psychological need. You cannot feel good about yourself without a sense of your own worth. All our inspirations are based on this fundamental need. Healthy self-esteem is the departing point for all kinds of love. You cannot love others if you do not love yourself first. According to the Bible, self-esteem is an imperative: "Love your neighbor as you love yourself." Matthew 22:39.

Low self-esteem is the root of much personal pain. It affects marriage, family, and consequently, society. People with low self-esteem feel isolated, unloved and defenseless. They are either overly aggressive or overly passive. They, therefore, find and offer little satisfaction in relationships.

People with high self-esteem are treated differently from those with low self-esteem. They are also more enjoyable to be with.

Following are some of the signs of low, poor or no self-esteem:
— Finding yourself in a thoroughly hostile environment where nobody likes you.
— Feeling bad about yourself and tending to be defensive when you are corrected.
— Using expressions like: "Nobody loves me," "I am useless," "I can't do anything right," "I'm a failure," "I cannot change."

But here is the good news: you can break the habit of feeling bad about yourself and improve your poor or low self-esteem.

ACCEPT YOURSELF AS YOU REALLY ARE

Self-acceptance is the key to positive self-esteem. A life without self-acceptance is a life in which a most basic human need goes unfulfilled.

Self-acceptance means you welcome yourself for being the person you are, not the person you should be. You never are as you should be. In reality you know you do not walk a straight path. There are many curves and many wrong decisions which, in the course of life, have brought you to where you are now.

When you accept yourself merely for what you do or have, you are not accepting yourself as you are. When you accept yourself for what you are, as a whole person, then your self-acceptance is real and total. To accept yourself as a person does not mean that you deny your defects, dwell on them, or try to explain them away. Self-acceptance does not mean everything you do is beautiful and fine. Only when you truly face your defects along with your virtues, will you really face your uniqueness.

Therefore, the first step for improving your self-worth is to honestly admit you have a low or poor self-esteem.

The second step is to recognize your defects and shortcomings. This is one of the hardest things for us to accept. To achieve this crucial feeling of acceptance of yourself — your flaws, limitations, moral imperfections and your sins — which will bring you an inner peace, you must realize that the absence of self-reconciliation is one of the greatest impediments to the quest for self-acceptance.

Consequently, the third step toward a high self-esteem is to experience a reconciliation with one's inner self. This happens by accepting yourself in your totality — both your goodness and your nastiness. Not that you identify with your negative side or succumb to it, but rather that you perceive and discover yourself as you actually are before God.

After that, and using your self-reconciliation as a departing point, start a change through a growing and maturing process. This could be the fourth step. To help you take this important step is the purpose of the next day.

TESTIMONIES

MIKE: "I like myself, yet my present job has caused me to realize I don't accept myself very well. I compare myself unfavorably with the other men. Even though my self-esteem has grown greatly, in times of stress I regress to being down on myself.

My low self-esteem is evident when I'm not able to be myself, to be open, honest and loving. Not speaking up and not knowing what I want for me, are evidences of my poor self-esteem.

At some level I don't believe I am worthy of having my own ideas and opinions. I am afraid to be a success. I am thankful I realize this and am working at it.

The most difficult thing to accept about myself is my lack of desire to really take a position on most things. I tend to drift along with the tide and take the non-controversial approach. I agree with people so they will like me rather than use my energy to accept and solve problems."

AMY: "I enjoy who I am and am grateful for my uniqueness and gifts. The satisfaction I find in cooking, my confidence in trying new recipes, the fun of making things for our home like the balloon shades, my yearning to learn more about the computer, all add to the excitement in my life because of who I am."

CHRISTINE: "I feel a special kind of peace since discovering more about who I am. I'm convinced I've been wishy-washy too long and I've finally been able to do what I felt was right for me.

I always did what every one else thought was right for me. Knowing I'm capable of making decisions for myself is liberating. It's so different from being concerned about what other people think of me. Now I can see how I may be able to like myself. But I can see where I've only just begun. I don't know where I'm going but I feel good. I'm confident I'm heading in the right direction."

QUESTIONS FOR REFLECTION

1. *Do I accept myself as I really am?*
   List a couple of positive and negative signs of self-acceptance.

75

2. *What do I find most difficult to accept about myself?*
   Why?
3. *Do I feel most people really like me?*
   Make a list of them. Ask yourself why they do.
4. *Are there any symptoms of low or poor self-esteem in my life?*
   Describe some of them.
5. *How do I feel about how I look?*
   List negative and positive feelings.
6. *Do I find it difficult to admit when I am wrong?*
   Reflect on a recent time when this happened?
7. *For what do I need to forgive myself?*
   Forgiveness of self is a requisite for giving and receiving forgiveness.

GROWING AND MATURING

GROWING

Deep inside, each of us wants to be more, and to grow as a person.

Traditionally, the term personal growth meant 'perfection of self, self-mastery, and self-denial.' Today, "personal growth" means self-development, self-fulfillment and self-identity. Simply, it is a dynamic process for becoming fully human.

The potential for growth we have in almost all areas of human endeavor is enormous. Actually, all human beings, regardless of age or circumstances, can grow in a healthy direction their entire life. But while all of us have the potential to lead rich and satisfying lives, few of us develop as much as we'd like. Many reasons account for this. Growth involves change and change from the old way to a new way is a complex process requiring hard work.

The growth of a person is comparable to a seed that germinates and begins to grow, hidden in the earth. One day a green shoot appears above ground and continues to grow because of the activity which is continuing underground, out of sight. Our growth is similar. It begins at a level which is hidden and continues there.

You cannot do anything to grow. What you can do is provide the conditions in which the innate principle or movement of life can operate. In the case of flowers, trees and crops, you provide a soil which has the right minerals. You also make sure they get sufficient water and heat. If the right conditions are not provided they fail to grow even though you want them to. Similarly, it is not enough to intend to grow as a person. It is necessary to provide the right conditions. Then our body grows, our mind grows, and our person grows.

Indeed, you have the potential to grow not just physically — that's automatic — but also mentally, to the fullness, integrity and maturity of yourself. And that depends almost completely on your personal decision and effort. Personal growth is the result of education received from outside ourself and our effort.

To grow is a permanent challenge of life. The ever-changing seasons are constant reminders to us that to be alive is to be changing. No two moments are ever alike. Life involves movement. Static life without movement soon dies. Life is a process, a journey, a dynamic activity — or it is nothing at all.

Growing is the most wonderful process in Creation.

MATURING

We hurt ourselves and others not because we are bad, but because we are immature. Selfishness, self-centeredness and childishness are the signs of immaturity in a person. The basic challenge of each person is to become more mature.

According to experts, the failure of education is that it does not provide a way for the person to realize their potential hidden within them. Many difficulties in personal life and relationships are due to the lack of the person's development to maturity. And this is because of the failure to understand that development is a growth process and not a formation process. In other words, to mature we need to learn by experiencing more than we need to learn intellectually.

To mature is to grow psychologically inside one's self. This happens when we face our reality, our failures, our responsibilities and our commitments. To mature means to assume responsibility for ones self. It supposes a harmonic development of the person — a real interior unity. It is an integration of the emotional, intellectual, and volitional elements in a person so he/she acts responsibly by facing reality and involving him/herself in life.

Maturity is unselfishness and unself-centeredness. Selfishness and self-centeredness produce a variety of conditions which prevent you from functioning to your full potential. They prevent your personal growth. Among such conditions are guilt, anxiety, stress, depression, anger, frustration. Maturity, on the other hand, is the ability to deal with those conditions, control and handle them.

A mature person is one who can live in an objective and reasonable way, not according to emotional reactions. A mature person, in practice, is one who is grown-up inside, and not at the mercy of negative and destructive forces within them. A mature person is someone who grows and improves in his/her thinking, judging, discerning, feeling, wanting, loving and serving.

Finally, I would like to state that maturity is not directly connected to age. It does not depend on having lived a certain number of years. This is very clear from seeing that some people are still immature at forty or sixty, and others are quite mature at twelve, fifteen or twenty, though this is very rare.

AS A MARRIED PERSON

Maturity is the ability to live in peace with those people and things we cannot change.

If you, as a married person, want to grow and mature, the first step you have to take is to define your goals in your married life. To do so, honestly answer these or similar questions:

- Personally, what am I aiming for in our marriage?
- What are my main goals in our married life?
- In all honesty, how accurately or quickly am I moving toward them?

You can find personal growth and maturity when your main goal is a positive and creative relationship with your spouse. In fact, there is no such thing as an isolated person. It is only through achieving a relationship of the best kind that you will grow to your full personal maturity. Conversely, the inability to achieve this interpersonal relationship is the root of all the self-destructive tendencies in human nature. That's why we can conclude that the affirmation of life, growth and maturity all depend on the capacity to relate on a person-to-person basis.

This type of growth necessarily implies commitment. In this sense marriage is not the only relationship of this kind. For most ordinary people, though, it is the one which offers the best chance for growth and, at the same time, serves other vital, important social purposes.

Is there any more stimulating challenge to personal development than a commitment to share life with a chosen person of the opposite sex? The challenges, responsibilities and privileges of this way of life may be difficult and even dangerous, but it could be the first step to grow and mature as a married person.

Your second step could be to go to work on your marriage relationship by experiencing a loving reconciliation through an honest giving and receiving of forgiveness and peace.

Are you ready? Say nothing. Just keep reading with an open heart.

TESTIMONIES

BRIAN: "In many ways I am an immature person, yet I feel grateful for the growth I've experienced.

79

I am thrilled at how I've handled my new responsibilities. And I'm even happier that I'm moving toward more growth and maturity.

"I need to grow in the following ways:
— Accept myself better as I am.
— Accept and assume responsibility for myself.
— Stick my neck out more and assume reasonable risks.
— Improve my personal relationship with you."

CAROL: "I have a need to be taken care of that's not healthy for me. It causes me to be critical of you and that's not fair. I see my selfishness and self-centeredness when I hang on to resentment and have a "poor me" attitude. It's like feeling jealous of your newly found success on the job.

I want to find fault with you and say you're putting the job before me, yet I know in my heart that's not true. But it surely makes an easy cop-out for me so I won't have to see my shortcomings and change me."

JULIETT: "It is easy for me to be there for other people, but I need to grow in being more independent. I need to take care of me better so I don't rely on other people for my feelings of self worth.

It's hard for me to accept myself where I am when it's not where I want to be. I keep thinking I'll be happy when . . . he changes, we have more money, I can quit work, the operation is over, the weather gets better, etc. And that's not being realistic. I need to grow to enjoy every day because of who I am, to see the goodness in me."

QUESTIONS FOR REFLECTION

1. *Are there any symptoms of selfishness or self-centeredness in my life?*
   Please list them.
2. *Do I consider myself a mature person?*
   Why?
3. *Am I growing as a person?*
   Reflect on and list the concrete ways.
4. *In what ways do I especially need to grow?*
   Be specific.
5. *What are the right and the necessary conditions for me to grow and mature as a married person?*
   Think about and list.
6. *What are my actual goals in my married life?*
   Am I following them?
7. *Truthfully, how is my personal relationship with my spouse?*
   Describe in loving detail.

EXPERIENCING RECONCILIATION

REACHING OUT BEYOND YOURSELF

If you do not want to lock yourself up in a vicious circle of pride, narcissism, selfishness and self-centeredness, you must reach out beyond yourself.

During the previous days of journeying toward your inner self to find identity, you have realized that:

- You are a unique person but imperfect and incomplete.
- You have masks that cover your real self.
- You have precious values but also deep needs.
- You have an inner potential but, at the same time, many limitations.
- You cannot live for yourself because you strongly need to love and to be loved.

In other words, you are discovering you are not an island. For this reason you have to communicate deeply and share from within with your closest partner in your life — your spouse.

How can you initiate this profound communication and sharing?

Reconciliation is the only door for a deep communication between two persons. It is the surest way to inner peace and happiness. You cannot know each other, understand each other, or grow in intimacy and love if you don't practice frequent reconciliation. Reconciliation is the normal process of growing more intimate with each other. And because it is only those we love deeply that we can hurt deeply, reconciliation is the necessary first step toward genuine love.

Wherever did we get the idea that if we love someone we won't hurt them? How can two people be bound together freely in an intimate relationship, daring to share all their thoughts, feelings and attitudes, without sharing some of the heartache, loneliness and sinfulness that's inside? As a matter of fact, the very wounds and scars from your intimate battles become signs of victory through your reconciliation.

81

True reconciliation is the test of the authenticity of your honesty, self-awareness, self-identity and self-realization.

But what is reconciliation all about?

ASKING FORGIVENESS

A few years ago a sentence from the novel and movie, "Love Story," was quite popular. It said "To love someone is to never have to say 'I'm sorry'!" That is a very superficial concept and experience of love.

True love is having to say "I'm sorry," or "I was wrong," or "Will you forgive me?" as soon as it is necessary. All those or similar sayings are powerful healers of genuine love.

It is hard to say "I'm sorry, I made a mistake," or "I am at fault." But such self-honesty and self-responsibility inspires self-growth. To say "I'm sorry" without blaming or implicating the partner requires magnanimity and gentleness. It reaffirms one's commitment to remain in a healthy and loving relationship.

Hardest of all is to say "Please forgive me." Because to ask forgiveness is to become vulnerable and needy. It gives the power of rejection to your partner. It is asking your spouse to give you something you do not deserve, merit or win. Your spouse could reasonably refuse. In these cases it would be good to remember that forgiveness is not, after all, a matter of your mind; it is a matter of your heart. It is easier to say "I love you" than to say "I'm sorry," but it is less effective. This is essentially true when your spouse is deeply wounded by you.

According to my personal experience, through all my years of ministry to and with married couples, when trouble comes to a marriage, both spouses owe the other an apology. Reconciliation begins only when someone makes an apology, means it, then lives it.

There is no other way to effective reconciliation.

GRANTING FORGIVENESS

After you ask forgiveness of your spouse and receive it, you will be ready to grant your pardon.

To give forgiveness means to accept your partner in his/her totality, both their goodness and nastiness. And to accept his/her reality, without distortions, blind spots, self-rejection or smug complacency. To give forgiveness is at the heart of your relationship with each other. A broken relationship, healed by forgiveness, will not return to its previous state. It will improve, and consequently both of you will change deeply.

It is out of the hurt and disillusionment that you can leap beyond the hurt through forgiveness.

In this sense the following verses from Patrick P. Donnelly are enlightening:

"Perhaps the hardest lesson life teaches is that shared pain is as important as shared laughter; that tears shed together mingle more intimately and have greater effect than do bodies in the act of love...

"That the agony of our lives, shared with those we love for peace and contentment, are found not in the beginning of things but at the end...

"And the reality of our humanity is that the joy of the young and the healthy is illusion. Only the calm joining of scattered bodies and battered souls is reality."

Unconditional forgiveness is definitely an essential part of unconditional love. But unconditional forgiveness is impossible without the power of God.

TESTIMONIES

NEAL: "My biggest failure in my relationship with Lucy, as in the rest of my life, is my habit of not assuming responsibility. I do what I must when my back is up against the wall. But I will slough off my responsibilities on her, or others, whenever I can."

LUCY: "I must stop trying to be a perfectionist. I should listen more to Neal and try to respond to his needs and expectations. I should make more time for him."

MIKE: "I need to ask forgiveness from my spouse for my stubbornness, my inability to show my love, and how fragile I am. I also have to ask her loving help: to overcome my tendency to procrastinate, my lack of self-control with my temper and eating habits, and my lack of thoughtfulness at times."

ELAINE: "It's so comforting to know it's natural to hurt someone you love. I always thought I was really bad if I hurt someone, as unintentional as it was. This really makes sense and frees me up to be myself.

I never thought about apologizing because I could always justify my behavior by blaming my spouse. "If it wasn't for him, I'd be okay." But apologizing brings a wonderful healing to our relationship.

I am grateful for the knowledge that I'm the only one I can change."

JESSICA: "I am insecure and worry about unimportant things like the impatience that I sometimes feel; my selfishness in wanting to spend my evenings doing my own thing rather than talking with him; my preoccupation with the children; my tendency to hide my true feelings, especially anger; my mistakes in the past . . . All this and more need his loving forgiveness, his understanding, and his help and encouragement.

Definitely, I need to experience a loving reconciliation with him."

RECONCILIATION TIME

At the end of this Second Week, when both of you have finished your reading, reflecting and writing in your notebooks, is the time for reconciliation.

How can you do it?

Here is a suggested guide. Feel free to use your creativity to change it as you desire.

I. FIND SOME PLACE in your home or outside where the two of you can communicate and share calmly and intimately.

II. LIGHT A CANDLE, a symbol of your eagerness for honesty, mutual knowledge, love and peace.

III. BE SILENT for 20 to 30 minutes to prepare yourselves for your reconciliation. During this time write your personal answers to the following points:

1. IN WHAT WAYS DO I THINK I HAVE FAILED IN MY RELATIONSHIP WITH YOU?

2. BECAUSE OF THIS I NEED YOU TO FORGIVE ME FOR . . .

3. AM I HARBORING RESENTMENTS ABOUT SOMETHING YOU HAVE FAILED TO APOLOGIZE ABOUT?

4. WHAT IS THE PART I HAVE PLAYED IN MAKING OUR COMMUNICATION DIFFICULT?

5. FINALLY, IN REGARD TO THIS SECOND WEEK, I WOULD LIKE TO SHARE WITH YOU . . .

IV. GET TOGETHER and give each other a sign of tenderness and affection — like kisses, hugs, caresses — and look into each other's eyes with confidence and love.

VII. SHARE YOUR ANSWERS TO THE FIVE PREVIOUS POINTS, ONE BY ONE, AND WITHOUT INTERRUPTIONS.

VIII.CLOSE YOUR TIME TOGETHER with affirmative and encouraging comments, including spontaneous signs of loving gratitude and peace.

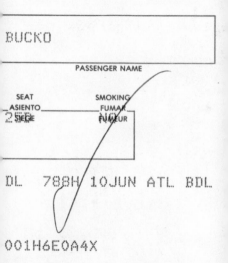

BUCKO

PASSENGER NAME

SEAT
ASIENTO   SMOKING
25E   FUMAR
SIEGE   NO
             FUMEUR

DL 788H 10JUN ATL BDL

001H6E0A4X

Is God Alive In Our Marriage?

Third Week

IS GOD ALIVE IN OUR MARRIAGE?

First Day   **AWAKENING**

Second Day   **ASKING YOURSELF ABOUT GOD**

Third Day   **SEARCHING FOR GOD TOGETHER**

Fourth Day   **LISTENING TO GOD'S WORD**

Fifth Day   **DISCOVERING GOD'S VISION ABOUT MARRIAGE**

Sixth Day   **ENCOUNTERING GOD IN MARRIAGE**

Seventy Day   **PRAYING TOGETHER AS A COUPLE**

"Stand Up; I Want To Talk To You!"

The Book Of Ezekiel 2:1.

STOP!

THIS WEEK COULD BE VERY DIFFICULT FOR SOME BECAUSE WE ARE GOING TO DEAL WITH THE ESSENCE OF FAITH: THE MYSTERY OF GOD.

THERE ARE MANY MYSTERIES IN LIFE: LIFE ITSELF, DEATH, LIGHT AND DARKNESS, GOOD AND EVIL, GAL-AXIES . . .

NOW, YOU ARE INVITED TO KEEP READING, REFLECT-ING, EXPERIENCING AND SHARING.

THIS WEEK IS ROOTED IN THE EXPERIENCE OF MIL-LIONS OF HUMAN BEINGS THROUGHOUT HISTORY WHO GIVE TESTIMONY WITH THEIR LIVES OF THAT VERY IMPORTANT PRINCIPLE:

WE, AS HUMAN BEINGS, CANNOT BECOME HAPPY PEOPLE WITHOUT GOD. WE CANNOT SATISFY OUR INNERMOST NEED AND LONGING FOR LOVE, HAR-MONY, PERFECTION, AND CONSEQUENTLY, FOR PEACE AND JOY, WITHOUT GOD.

GOD CREATED US TO BECOME TRULY HAPPY.

GOD IS NOT AN IDEA OR A CONCEPT.

GOD IS NOT A LUXURY.

GOD IS THE SOLID AND NECESSARY FOUNDATION

FOR A HAPPY MARRIED LIFE.

ENCOURAGING TESTIMONIES

• "This has been the first time we have seriously reflected and shared about God's place in our marriage. We finally found the 'key' that we were looking for many years ago."—James.

• "Reading the Word of God in connection with our marriage has been a fascinating revelation and like a conversion for both of us. We have discovered that we have not given 'top priority' to the Lord in our relationship."—Marilyn.

• "I found it difficult to realize that we did not give 'top priority' to the Lord in our marriage. From now on we do not want to have any more fear or confusion. We will deepen more and more our relationship with the Lord."—William.

• "This was a wonderful and yet painful week. We really experienced God's presence in each other and the oneness in our marriage. After hours of dialogue, we shared a closeness and joy much more intense than ever before. We believe that since that night, we both are realizing that our relationship seems much more solid. It was difficult for me because I wanted him to be open, but at the same time I was not sure I wanted to hear what I heard. Really, the secret was the mysterious presence of the Lord and His powerful action among us. That was something very special . . ."—Suzanne.

• "This week has been a discovery: the unity we have is a clear and precious gift from God's Heart."—Peter.

• "The revelation of God's Plan for us, is the most precious gift we both have received in our 17 years of married life."—Ray.

• "Sharing on a deep level has brought us closer together. I can really feel the Lord's presence in our relationship and I can see our marriage as a living Sacrament. I'm so grateful to God for opening my eyes."—Tracey.

• "I see God's Plan for us is to live our marriage as a couple, devoted to loving, believing in, and caring for one another. God's Plan of unity gives us strength and confidence in each other and in our relationship. This is why I find it easier for me to resist the 'world's plan' and instead reach out to you so that we can make God's Will a reality for us."—Stan.

• "During this week He told us to fortify ourselves with prayer to keep us going in time of need and that we always have Him in our midst. We can pray together before retiring, and we can do more Bible dialogue to improve our relationship with God."—Al.

The
FIRST DAY

AWAKENING

LISTENING FROM WITHIN

The lack of meaning in life, usually accompanied by a feeling of emptiness, is a widespread phenomenon of our times. Our high-tech consumaristic society is continually creating material needs, but at the same time is unable to satisfy our basic need for a deep meaning in our lives. The message we hear is that we will be happy if we have a higher standard of living: a good salary, a better career, a bigger and more comfortable home, luxurious vacations, etc. However, the more material things we attain the deeper our emptiness becomes.

If you are honest with yourself, you will admit that deep down inside yourself there is an emptiness that needs to be fulfilled. Your heart yearns for something beyond yourself. There is a void that earth cannot satisfy nor fulfill. You are realizing that the greatest need you have is a spiritual awakening.

In a world filled with materialism there is a need for a revival of Faith. The revival must be experienced within the innermost you:

> beginning in your mind
> following in your heart and will
> invading your whole being.

This spiritual awakening, this revival of Faith, is a free gift from heaven, but you can do something. You can prepare yourself to receive this Grace by opening up your mind completely. How?

By reflecting carefully on some of the following rational statements. They have become famous throughout history and have enlightened many honest and humble people.

Ready?

LISTENING FROM WITHOUT

VOLTAIRE: "If God did not exist it would be necessary to invent Him, but all nature cries aloud that He does exist, that there is a supreme intelligence, an immense power, an admirable order, and everything teaches us our own dependence on it."

KIERKEGAARD: "If God does not exist it would, of course, be impossible to prove it; and if He does exist it would be folly to attempt it."

TERTULIAN: "God is invisible, although seen; incomprehensible, although revealed by grace; unfathomable, although fathomed by the human senses."

CHRYSOSTOM: "Comprehended God is no God."

EINSTEIN: " 'God is the order in the universe.' The most beautiful thing we can experience is the mystery."

SPINOZA: "God is absolutely first cause. Therefore, God necessarily exists."

AQUINAS: "Everything moves. Whatever moves is moved by another. Therefore, there must be something which is unmoved-mover. This is God."

ARISTOTLE: "All philosophy should orient itself toward the concept of God. If it does not, it doesn't deserve the name . . . Man has to return to God in order to be fulfilled."

SCOUTUS: "We do not know what God is because He is infinite and therefore, objectively unknowable."

DE LA BRUYERE: "The fact it is impossible for me to prove there is no God proves to me His existence. I feel that there is a God, and I do not feel that there is none. This satisfies me. All the reasoning in the world is useless. I conclude there is God!"

BERGSON: "God may be the source of the 'elan vital' " (Life).

SWEDENBORG: "Conscience is God's presence in man." "We are because God is." "God is our home."

PASCAL: "There are only three kinds of persons: those who serve God having found Him. Others who are occupied in seeking Him, not having found Him. While the remainder live without seeking Him, and without having found Him.

92

The first are reasonable and happy.
The last are foolish and happy.
Those between are unhappy and unreasonable.
It is the heart which experiences God, and not reason."

FROMM: "Theologians and philosophers have been saying for a century that God is Dead, but what we confront is the possibility that man is dead, transformed into a thing."

TILLICH: "The fundamental symbol of our ultimate concern is God. It is always present in any act of faith, even if the act of faith includes the denial of God."

Atheism, consequently, can only mean an attempt to remove any ultimate concern, to remain unconcerned about the meaning of one's existence.

Indifference toward the ultimate question is the only imaginable form of atheism."

LUDWIF: "In practice all men are atheists. They deny their faith by actions."

THOREAU: "Blessed are they who never read a newspaper for they shall see nature, and through her, God."

SAINT PAUL: "In Him we have life, movement and being."

SAINT AUGUSTIN: "You have made us for yourself, Lord, and our heart can find no rest until it rest in you!"

REFLECTING

1. *Which one of the previous statements touched me the most?*
2. *Why?*
3. *What does God mean to me?*

ASKING YOURSELF ABOUT GOD

GOD?

God! Is there any God? Who is God? Is God alive? Where is God? How can God be found? Is God a problem to solve or a mystery to live? These and similar questions are as old as mankind is.

The purpose of this day is precisely to help you to deal with these transcendental questions by asking yourself about God, to discover Him from your own experience of life. It will not be an easy task because we are living in a materialistic society where everybody is so busy and concerned about themselves that it is a luxury to think about God.

According to many of today's theologians, atheism is the most serious phenomenon of our times. What are the atheists like?

They are just like other people. But they deny the reality of God's existence. They do not want God to exist.

There are two kinds of atheists: **positive,** who deny God with arguments and behaviors; and **practical,** who, even though they say they believe in God with words, deny Him by living as if God doesn't exist. Atheism is a problem not only of the mind but also of the will.

The word "atheism" sounds strong to many of today's men and women, so they prefer to call themselves "agnostics" to express their religious situation and behavior more gently. What are agnostics like? They are ordinary people. They think that nothing can be affirmed nor denied about God, consequently they do not miss God. Practically, the so called agnostics are atheists and unbelievers too.

What are true believers like? In general, they are the ones who having honestly asked themselves about God, encounter Him and have a personal relationship with Him. To ask oneself about God is a key step in everybody's life.

94

THE QUESTION ABOUT GOD

In life, everybody is looking for answers but very few find them. Why?

Because, before any answer there must be a question.

Therefore, if you want to find the right answer you have to ask yourself the right question.

Then you will find the right answer within you.

In fact, we humans, as intelligent beings, are able to question everything, because everybody is a living question to themselves and to others. On the other hand, the question about God is not something arbitrary; it springs up from the innermost personal reality of every man and woman. The question about God is the most fundamental and radical question of all, because all questions of life are rooted in the question about God.

According to the Bible, man and woman, willingly or unwillingly, consciously or unconsciously, are always related and united to God. He is the Creator.

We urgently need to question ourselves about God as the meaning of our existence, if we do not want to renounce our human dignity and destroy ourselves.

HOW TO ASK YOURSELF ABOUT GOD

To answer the question about God, we must first ask ourselves another question: "What is the greatest aspiration of most people today?" According to many experts, the number one question for many people is how to improve their living standard and quality of life. More concretely: how to increase the economic level of their lives.

Answering questions about economics, quality of life, ethics and the meaning of life, bring us closer to each other as we struggle together for social justice, the common-good, and peace.

Therefore, the process to ask yourself the question about God could be by not starting with the high clouds of theoretical ideas and concepts, but from the deepness of your own living experience of life, and your inner desire to grow and improve your standard or quality of life.

Then, you could ask yourself about:
1. The quality of your life.
2. The meaning of your daily life.
3. The ultimate and total sense of life.

Finally, at this point in time, you will be able and ready to question about God. Do not ask about God until you have questioned yourself about the meaning of your life, that is rooted in the mystery of God.

At the bottom of today's most radical questions there is the unanswered question about God. If you do not deal with that transcendental question, you will be unable to answer the other important questions.

Believing or not believing, that is the question!

REFLECTING

1. *Does my life have meaning?*
2. *Why?*
3. *What and how do I feel about God right now?*

The
Third Day

SEARCHING FOR GOD TOGETHER

WE HAVE LOST GOD

A hundred years ago, a German philosopher, Friedrich Nietzche wrote in his book Zarathustra: "God is dead!"

In our century, the famous American psychologist Eric Fromm, in his address to the American Orthopsychiatric Association, in San Francisco, April 16, 1966, said: "Theologians and philosophers have been saying for a century that 'God is dead,' but what we confront is the possibility that 'man is dead' transformed into a thing, a producer, a consumer, an idolator, or other things.

In other words, God is alive because we cannot die. He is Himself, the Source of Life. What happened is that we humans have lost Him in the atheism of our own hearts. Preoccupied with having and doing, we have forgotten our being, and consequently we have lost God, our Creator.

In fact, most of today's married couples seem to give maximum importance to material things, and behave as if material things — cars, houses, clothing, money, etc. — were the most meaningful thing in their life. They are materialistic people who experience a degree of repugnance at the thought of accepting anything which is not material.

This way, the day-by-day-life for most married people is technical. They depend to a very high degree upon machines. Their way is to obtain material results in the quickest possible way. Consequently, superficiality or lack of interior content or depth constitutes another feature of contemporary couples. The lack of inner contentment and peace makes them live in an artificial environment. They are attracted to triviality. They make themselves insensitive to the presence of transcendental values. They are alienated from the source of all meaningful value — God the supreme and absolute value. He is the Mystery of Mysteries!

The result of this superficiality and inauthentic existence is loneliness. That is why, frequently, married people who live together, feel alone and like strangers to each other. This estrangement leads to an attitude of suspicion. This makes one see the partner as an opponent or competitor, and sometimes, as a prospective enemy. Business becomes more important than homes and churches. This practical atheism or indifference makes God irrelevant for many couples and families. God is not seen in the horizon nor in the bottom of their lives. He is eclipsed, or perhaps forgotten, or lost.

RETURNING TO GOD AS A COUPLE

If you have lost God, what can you do? You could do as the two people who got lost in a jungle. Looking for the way out, they met each other and realized that both had the same problem and need. They decided to seek the way out together. Of course, they found it.

In the jungle of today's society, the need to search for truth, love, justice and peace is common to husbands and wives. Also common to them is the need for an absolute and infinite reality — God. Why not decide to search together, hand-in-hand, as a married couple?

How To Do It

According to Scripture, man and woman are the gift of the divine, created by God. So man and woman are accepted and loved by God, first. This acceptance by God is the source of all love. All other human love is derived from this source.

How Can Husband and Wife Experience God's Love

First, in the very act of personal existence, by remembering that God is Love.

Second, in the intense drama of our personal life in which God is more than a mere spectator.

Third, in the returning to Him under His own attraction and initiative. This return to Him answers God's original call into existence.

Genuine married love is always a pilgrimage and a process. You never arrive. You're continually returning to God.

Surely, your married life is built upon an eternal triangle. At the bottom of the triangle are husband and wife. At the top is God. If you are united at the top, you cannot separate at the bottom.

98

If you are faithful and persevere in searching honestly for God, you will find Him in the deepest level of yourself and will realize that both of you are with God and God with You.

Then you will have a new exciting experience: that you, as a married couple, are not any more just two, but three.

And He will be Number One in your marriage and family life. That's an exciting experience.

REFLECTING

1. *Am I satisfied with our married life?*
   Why?
2. *Are we searching for God together, as a married couple?*
   Explain your answer, please.
3. *If we have lost God, can we return to Him?*
   How?

The
Fourth Day

LISTENING TO GOD'S WORD

LISTENING TO GOD

The true search for God is like when you receive a visitor: after you sit down, you listen.

God actually is not something that you can buy, but someone who comes to you, to speak to you. When someone comes, the first thing you do is to sit down and listen. This could be the main attitude in your looking for God.

According to theologians, God speaks to us in many mysterious and marvelous ways:

— Through the Creation — His Work.
— Through our conscience — His Voice.
— Through the circumstances of our lives — His Will.
— Through the sufferings and needs of our neighbors — His Call.
— Through the Bible — His Living Word.

The Bible is the key to listen to God and discern what He is telling us through other ways. In fact, the finest men and women in the history of salvation have found and experienced God in their lives by listening to His Living Word in the Sacred Scriptures.

GOD'S WORD

The Living Word of God varies according to the capacity of the listener. God portrays His Message in many colors, so that whoever gazes upon It can see in It what suits him or her. Within It He has buried many treasures, so that each of us might become rich in seeking them out.

The Word of God is a supernatural light. It is projected upon us to help us discern what He is telling us throughout our lives. It is also a supernatural energy that enables us to do whatever He wants.

The Word of God is the testimony of His revelation. It bridges the abyss which separates us from Him, making us a part of Himself: of His knowledge, of His love and His life. It starts a personal encounter with us.

Each encounter with God, through His Living Word, is distinct and unique. Each encounter with God is a deep move from Him — who takes the initiative — to us, by going from His Infiniteness to our limitations, from His Grace to our disgrace, from His Light to our darkness, from His Power to our weakness, from His Love to our selfishness, from His Peace to our anxiety, from His Joy to our sadness, from His Happiness to our unhappiness . . .

READING GOD'S WORD

To read the Bible is not easy. You cannot assume that because you have learned to read, you are ready to read the Bible. The Bible is not just a book to be read, it is a Living Word to be listened to. How can you read the Bible so you will be able to listen to the Word of God?

There are many ways to read. We will concentrate on two: material, or informational reading, and spiritual, or reflective. We may use one or the other depending on our personal intention, purpose and attitude. Material reading is just for the sake of gaining information. When you read this way, you are using a **quantity** approach, i.e., you try to learn as much as quickly as you can. In spiritual reading, the **quality** of your reading is most important. It is not how much you read, but rather how well.

In reading information, you often race against time; you tend to be very critical and analytical. Reflective reading is done much more leisurely; you forget the ticking of your watch. Usually in informational reading you control the situation. Spiritual reading is a time of meditation; you wait patiently for the message to unfold before you. The goal of informational reading is pretty concrete; it is usually functional; it is to develop certain expertise. In spiritual reading the goal is a meditative attitude and openness to the transforming message of the spirit. This type of receptivity involves risk and trust, but enables you to move into a deeper meaning of life.

To read the Bible and to listen to the Word of God requires spiritual reading. You have to read not just with your head but with your heart and your soul.

What can you do when you do not understand the Word of God, even though you have tried to listen with your heart and soul? Be glad and do not be saddened. You have been challenged by God's Word. So listen and listen again. People are happy when they are drinking. They are not depressed because they cannot exhaust the spring. Let the spring of God's Word quench your thirst and not your thirst quench the spring.

God's Word is a mysterious treasure. Whenever you discover some part of the treasure, don't think you have exhausted God's Word.

REFLECTIVE READING

"With a large crowd gathering and people from every town finding their way to Him, Jesus used this parable:

'A sower went out to sow his seed. As he sowed, some fell on the edge of the path and was trampled on; and the birds of the air ate it up.

Some seed fell on rock, and when it came up it withered away, having no moisture.

Some seed fell among thorns and thorns grew with it and choked it.

And some seed fell into rich soil and grew and produced its crop a hundredfold.

Saying this He cried, 'Listen, anyone who has ears to hear!'

His disciples asked Him what this parable might mean, and He said,

'This, then, is what the parable means: the seed is the word of God.

Those on the edge of the path, are people who have heard it, and then the devil comes and carries away the word from their hearts in case they should believe and be saved.

Those on the rock are people who, when they first hear it, welcome the word with joy. But these have not root; they believe for a while, and in time of trial they give up.

102

As for the part that fell into thorns, this is people who have heard, but as they go on their way they are choked by the worries and riches and pleasures of life and do not reach maturity.

As for the part in the rich soil, this is people with a noble and generous heart who have heard the word of God and take it to themselves and yield a harvest through their perseverance.' "

Luke 8:4-15.

REFLECT: What kind of soil am I at this time?

DISCOVERING GOD'S VISION
ABOUT MARRIAGE

BRAINSTORM

The purpose of this Fifth Day is to help you to prepare yourself to listen to God revealing His marvelous plan and vision about marriage.

But before you open the Bible, try to reflect on some of the following questions:

- Is unity between husband and wife something important and essential to their nature and constitution?
- Is marriage meaningful and worthwhile?
- What is the essence of married life?
- What is the main purpose of marriage?
- What is the true philosophy of marriage?
- Is marriage just a human institution built upon casual circumstances — sociological, psychological and economical — or is it a divine and sacred one?
- Are husband and wife absolutely independent and self-sufficient in marriage, or are they strongly rooted in God and dependent on Him, who is the Creator?
- Is there a divine plan for marriage?
- What is God's Vision about marriage?
- Is it important for husband and wife to live according to God's Vision and Plan?
- Does God want married people happy?
- Is happiness in marriage possible without God?
- Are there some outlines for a healthy and happy marriage life in the Bible?

To find the answers to each one of those or similar questions, try to read with your mind, your heart and your soul the three first chapters of the Bible.

Let's go and do it at once!

THE BIBLE'S AMAZING REVELATION

God's revelation about marriage and family appears in the first pages of the Book of Genesis. According to Scripture scholars, there are two parallel stories or complementary accounts about Creation.

I. FROM THE FIRST STORY: Genesis 1:1-31.
- God Is The Creator:
  "In the beginning God created the heavens and the earth."
- Marriage Is The Culmination Of God's Creative Work:
  "God said, 'Let us make man in our own image, in the likeness of ourselves, and let them be the masters of the fish of the sea, the birds of heaven, the cattle, all the wild beasts and all the reptiles that crawl upon the earth'."
- Marriage Is The Living Image Of God:
  "God created man in the image of Himself, in the image of God He created him, male and female He created them."

II. FROM THE SECOND STORY: Genesis 2:4-25.
- Marriage Is A Community Of Life And Love;
  "God said, 'It is not good that man should be alone. I will make him a helpmate' . . . So God made the man fall into a deep sleep. And while he slept, He took one of his ribs and enclosed it in the flesh. God built the rib He had taken from the man into a woman, and brought her to the man."
- Marriage Is a Mystery Of Communion And Unity:
  "The man exclaimed: 'This at last is bone from my bones, and flesh from my flesh! This is to be called woman, for this was taken from man.' This is why a man leaves his father and mother and joins himself to his wife, and they become one body."

REFLECTIVE READING

At the end of the second chapter of Genesis, an obvious question arises: If according to God's revelation marriage is so perfect, how can we account for so much unhappiness — infidelity, separation, divorce and breakdown in marriage and family — in history and up to this very day? What happened in "the beginning?"

To find the right answer to this transcendental question, let us keep reading, reflecting and listening to the Word of God, in the third chapter of Genesis. It is about the temptation the just created married couple had, to emancipate themselves from God and become independent and self-sufficient.

"The serpent was the most subtle of all the wild beasts that God had made. It asked the woman, 'Did God really say you were not to eat from any of the trees in the Garden?'

The woman answered the serpent, 'We may eat the fruit of the trees in the garden, but of the fruit of the tree in the middle of the garden God said, 'You must not eat it, nor touch it, under pain of death.''

Then the serpent said to the woman, 'No! You will not die! God knows in fact that on the day you eat it your eyes will be opened and you will be like gods, knowing good and evil.'

The woman saw that the tree was good to eat and pleasing to the eye, and that it was desirable for the knowledge that it could give. So she took some of its fruit and ate it. She gave also to her husband who was with her, and he ate it. Then the eyes of both of them were opened and they realized that they were naked. So they sewed fig-leaves together to make themselves loincloths.

The man and his wife heard the sound of God walking in the garden in the cool of the day, and they hid from Him among the trees of the garden. But God called to the Man, 'Where are you?' He asked.

'I heard the sound of you in the garden' he replied. 'I was afraid because I was naked, so I hid.' 'Who told you that you were naked?' He asked. 'Have you eaten of the tree I forbade you to eat?' Then the man replied, 'It was the woman you put with me; she gave me the fruit, and I ate it.' Then God asked the woman, 'What is this you have done?' The woman replied, 'The serpent tempted me and I ate.''

". . . So God expelled them from the garden of Eden, to till the soil from which they had been taken.

A GOLDEN RULE ABOUT MARRIAGE

What could be the key to live married life according to God's Vision?

We have just discovered, through reading the Bible, that in God's Plan, marriage is two people created and called to become one, and with God.

Therefore, the golden rule could be:

- ALL THAT PROMOTES GENUINE UNITY BETWEEN HUSBAND AND WIFE AND BETWEEN THE MARRIED COUPLE AND GOD IS IN ACCORDANCE WITH GOD'S VISION AND PLAN.
- ALL THAT ENDANGERS, HINDERS OR CORRUPTS GENUINE UNITY BETWEEN HUSBAND AND WIFE AND BETWEEN THE MARRIED COUPLE AND GOD IS AGAINST GOD'S VISION AND PLAN.

If you are longing for a happy marriage and family life, just follow this golden rule.

The
Sixth Day

ENCOUNTERING GOD IN MARRIAGE

YOU ARE NOT ALONE IN YOUR MARRIAGE

Maybe, at this point in time, you have strong doubts again and wonder if unity in marriage is possible. Marriage according to God's Plan is not an impossible dream.

The purpose of this Sixth Day is to help you find the answers to these doubts and offer you the opportunity to know that you are not alone in your marriage, because God is with you, in a very special way. Even though you have not realized it yet, God was with you from the very day of your wedding until now. Therefore, you are invited to change the dualistic and secularistic mentality about marriage, the "just the two of us" thinking, and become hopefully aware of the presence and action of God in your marriage.

God is the First Dimension of your marriage.

How can you discover and experience God's presence in your marriage? We cannot find God or know Him on a natural level, all at once, but through our realities enlightened by the gift of Faith. Realities are events that come from God and lead to Him. Therefore, God has to be found, not in the clouds of our ideas, thoughts and imaginations, but in the depth of our beings and through our daily lived experiences. Our personal experiences predispose us to the world of God's Grace.

A traditional theological principle states that "Grace builds on nature." That is, the more people realize their reality and gifts, the more they become aware of God's presence and action in their lives. On the contrary, the more people live unaware of their reality and talents, the more they feel alone and unhappy.

Let us apply all this to the reality and gifts of married life, by realizing what marriage is all about and consequently, by living it accordingly.

107

MARRIAGE IS A COVENANT

Marriage is God's Idea. The Biblical concept of marriage as a covenant is central to an understanding of marriage under God. The underlying theme of marriage as a spiritual covenant is evident in many Scripture passages, as you can realize:

• A Love Story: "Your time had come. The time for love. I spread part of my cloak over you and covered your nakedness; I bound myself by oath, I made a covenant with you — it is the Lord Yahweh who speaks — and you became mine." Ezekiel 16:8.

• Unfaithfulness: "Denounce your mother, denounce her, for she is not my wife nor am I her husband. Let her rid her face of her whoring, and her breasts of her adultery, or else I will strip her naked, expose her as on the day she was born. I will make a wilderness of her, turn her into an arid land, and leave her to die of thirst . . ." "That is why I am going to lure her and lead her out into the wilderness and speak to her heart." Hosea 2:1-6 and 16.

• Forgiveness: "Come back, disloyal Israel — it is Yahweh who speaks — I shall frown on you no more, since I am merciful. I shall not keep my resentment forever."'

"Only acknowledge your guilt: How you have apostatized from Yahweh your God, how you have flirted with strangers and have not listened to my voice."

"If you wish to come back, Israel — it is Yahweh who speaks — it is to me you must return. Do away with your abominations and you will have no need to avoid me. If you swear, 'As Yahweh lives!' truthfully, justly and honestly, the nations will bless themselves by you, and glory in you." Jeremiah 3:12-13; 4:1-2.

• Unconditional Love: "For Zion was saying, 'Yahweh has abandoned me, the Lord has forgotten me.' Does a woman forget her baby at the breast, or fail to cherish the son of her womb? Yet even if these forget, I will never forget you. See, I have branded you on the palms of my hands." Isaiah 49:16-16.

Therefore, marriage is a covenant relationship. Husband and wife enter into a covenant with each other and with God. When the spouses live their marriage in accordance to God's Idea, they experience the mystery of God's love to His people.

According to God's revelation, the basics of the marriage relationship are: fidelity, trust and unconditional love. Unfaithfulness, selfishness and prostitution are the main failures.

THE SACRAMENT OF MARRIAGE

The essential dimension of marriage as a sacrament is the relationship between Jesus Christ and His Church. In the light of this relationship, Christian marriage is explained.

As Christians and believers, we celebrate and experience the presence and power of our God in Jesus Christ. As Christians and believers, we also need to recognize that this Presence and Power is within the relationship and covenant of marriage. It is a simple awareness of God working in, and through us. In the Roman Catholic tradition we state that the couple (husband and wife) are the continuing main ministers of the sacrament to each other and that the priest is the official witness to the ritual of the wedding.

It is difficult to quote one particular passage from scripture to prove that a marriage is a sacrament. But it is not difficult for a couple to recognize the presence and action of Christ Jesus in their Christian marriage.

A sacrament is a living sign of God's love. Jesus Christ is the embodiment, pledge, and "sign" of God's love for us. For example, in Paul's Letter to the Ephesians, Chapter 5, Paul compares marriage to the covenant relationship. He states that there is not just a contract between Christ and his people or his body. It is a covenant which has been sealed in His blood. So also in marriage, there is that mysterious bond and covenant between husband and wife. "Give way to one another in obedience to Christ." We are given the example of Christ himself: we are to give ourselves to each other just as Christ gave Himself in love for His people, His Church.

In First Corinthians, Paul refers to Marriage in the Lord. Again, it is a couple who makes the covenant with each other, "In the Lord." There is always the presence of that Power and Grace in their commitment, because of their Baptism or union with Jesus.

The married couple must realize there is a deep and holy dimension to their love and commitment. Just as we take for granted the beating of our hearts, or the breath of life within us, so the married couple must recognize their deep commitment and love for each other and make their covenant stronger. Thus they become aware that God is with them, and their strength is coming from Someone greater than themselves: God. The couple, by this covenant, become a sign not so much for themselves, but for others, who can then see and recognize the Power and Grace of God in their commitment and covenant.

BRINGING SPIRITUALITY INTO
YOUR MARRIAGE

Most married couples do not realize that God is present in their marital relationship; always ready to assist them with His special graces; to keep them whole and holy; and if it is necessary, to save their marriage. Other couples, even though they say they believe, in reality, they do not.

God's graces, His loving, powerful and visible actions, are not automatic or magic. They require both partners to look for God's help within themselves and cooperate with him as much as they can. This is precisely what marriage spirituality is all about.

Today, the notion of spirituality of any kind is frequently subject to misunderstanding. The term "spirituality" can smack of unreality: hours of prayer and studying the Bible; a dispensing of material things for the sake of "spiritual experiences or religious practices." It is important to **reject** the unreality of such misunderstanding and illusion. Spirituality cannot be divorced from daily life. For any authentic believer, "spirit" has to do with the real, everyday life, consciously lived within the guiding presence of the Spirit of God. Solid and healthy spirituality cannot be divorced from one's everyday lived experiences, interpersonal relationships and real events.

Marriage spirituality has to be rooted in everyday married life. Consequently, interpersonal communication and the relationship between husband and wife are the core of the spirituality of every married couple. In other words, the way to bring spirituality to your marriage and meet God at the core of your marriage, is by deepening and consciously living the reality of your person-to-person-communication and relationship as husband and wife.

What is special about the spirituality of married people is the fact that in marriage, the Biblical term "neighbor," refers first of all to one's spouse. But genuine love between husband and wife is inseparable from their relationship with God, personally and as a couple. How can anyone achieve a true and balanced intimacy with God if they are incapable of, or have not achieved, the same kind of balanced relationship with his/her "neighbor," the spouse? The quality of your presence to one another defines the quality of your presence to God. Marital spirituality is the new way of life you initiate, after discovering your marriage in the light of God.

The
Seventh Day

PRAYING TOGETHER AS A COUPLE

PRAYING

To believe is to pray. Faith leads to prayer as the river to the sea; like food nourishes our bodies, prayer nourishes our faith. If you truly believe, you will pray.

But, praying is a gift from God. You cannot pray unless God opens your mind, moves your heart and attracts you to Him. Paul said it this way:

"The Spirit, too, helps us in our weakness, for we do not know how to pray as we ought; but the Spirit Himself makes intercession for us with groanings that cannot be expressed in speech." Romans 8: 26-27.

Praying is not a magic tool to change God's mind and heart, but His gift to change our minds, hearts and wills. The key attitude in praying is not being concerned about one's personal benefit, but simply remaining in God's presence with humility of heart, trust and living faith.

Prayer has fruitful effects, but usefulness is not its purpose. It is like friendship: it offers many useful benefits, but if they are the sole purpose for cultivating a friend, there is really no friendship at all, only a business relationship. Prayer cannot be measured in terms of usefulness, that is, you may not 'get something out of it,' or come to a clear conclusion. Prayer can only be understood as a complete surrender to God — the absolute Lord.

Prayer is best when it is simple, and it is simple when it has only one purpose: to be with God and walk in His presence. Can a flower forget the stalk supporting it and giving it existence minute by minute? God is present in the inner self of every human creature and hence you can be in His presence when you look into yourself.

Actually, though, prayer has to be expressed through one's whole life. It is necessary to spend some time with God, to communicate and to dialogue with Him, like friends and lovers do. They reserve certain times when they do nothing but "be together," and communicate with each other, not as an obligation, but as a need.

111

COUPLE PRAYER LIFE

A personal relationship with God is essential and irreplaceable, but for married people it is not enough. God has special ways of calling and communicating with each married couple, as a couple.

Based on my experiences in my ministry with married couples, I have realized that most spouses pray as individuals, but few as couples. Isn't it strange that a married couple share all — house, meals, bed, work, play and their own bodies, desires and dreams, but not their personal relationship with God?

Why does this happen? I think that one of the most powerful reasons is the individualistic mentality about faith, God and religion so many people have. And, because a personal relationship with God is the most intimate experience one can share, we have a natural timidness toward sharing it. Sometimes it is because of fear. Frequently the difficulty originates in the diversity of the personal histories, sensibilities and education of each one of the partners. Sometimes, the difficulty comes from the fact that partners have different religions, or belong to different cultures.

Why pray as a couple? The answer, coming from couples who do, is strongly affirmative and enthusiastic. They explain that their marriage prayer life has enriched their personal lives and has transformed their marriage relationship by introducing them to a new and happier dimension.

According to the Holy Scriptures, the reason is simple and clear: "Have you not read that the Creator from the beginning made them male and female and that He said, 'This is why a man must leave his father and mother, and cling to his wife and the two become one body. They are no longer two, therefore, but one body. So then, what God has united, man must not divide." Matthew 19:4-7.

The Biblical conclusion is obvious: If you are married, you cannot separate your personal prayer from your married life. You are called to relate to God not just as two people, but as one married couple.

How can you relate and communicate with God as one?

FIVE PRACTICAL STEPS

To encourage you to relate to and communicate with God as a couple, I would like to gently suggest to you five practical steps. They are gradual, i.e., you cannot take the next step without fully experiencing the previous one. This is very important.

The common key to these five steps is to share in the presence of God, as a husband and wife. The unconditional departing point of each one of these steps, is the personal relationship and communication with God. Without this personal experience, marital sharing will be superficial, meaningless and empty.

About the fifth step — the most precious one — do not be surprised if after honestly trying it, you feel confused, lost and frustrated. This is its price. You both will need a great deal of humility and loving patience to take this step. God will give it to you, as His very special gift, after you deeply experience the other four steps. And, that will not happen overnight. Following are the five steps or degrees of conjugal communication "in the Lord."

First: SHARING A BIBLE PASSAGE, by reading it together, having a short period of silence and afterwards, sharing with each other your thoughts, feelings and personal reactions to the Word of God. No comments. Just a respectful and loving listening with the heart to each other in the presence of God.

Second: SHARING YOUR PERSONAL PRAYER LIFE, by exchanging with each other your personal relationship with God and your living experiences about life, death, love, peace, justice, calls, dreams, struggles, crises, truth, good, sex, evil, temptations, ideals, beauty, deep needs, gifts etc.

Third: EVALUATING YOUR CONJUGAL LIFE, by reviewing it in the light of the Holy Scriptures, according to the "signs of the times," to discern what the Lord is telling you through the ordinary and extraordinary events of your personal, married, and family life.

Fourth: REVIEWING YOUR CONJUGAL COMMITMENT, by reexamining your commitment of being a testimony of love and unity: at your home, at work, in the neighborhood, in the Church, in your community and everywhere.

Fifth: PRACTICING MUTUAL EXHORTATION, by dialoguing in God's presence about each other's personal conduct and behavior with true honesty and love, to encourage each other to live and grow according to God's Will.

113

LET US PRAY TOGETHER

This is the Seventh Day of the Third Week. It is a wonderful opportunity for both of you to pray together as a couple and to experience God's presence and action in your midst. This way you will prepare yourselves to start the Fourth Week with the greatest guarantee of success.

You could follow this simple outline:

1. While sitting together — to feel each other's closeness and warmth — **spend some time in silence,** to become aware of God's presence with you.

2. **Listen together** to a short passage from the Bible, while one of you reads it aloud slowly.

3. **Pause** and let the Word of God silently sink into you, for a couple minutes.

4. **Tell** each other, as briefly as possible, what God's Word means to you.

5. **More silence.**

6. **Speak spontaneously and directly to God,** even if it is only "Thank You, Lord!" "Stay with us!" or "Lord, bless us!" or "We trust in You, Lord!"

7. In any case, you could hold hands and simply join your voices to say: "OUR FATHER . . ."

Are We
Becoming
One?

Fourth Week

ARE WE BECOMING ONE?

First Day   **STRENGTHENING OUR MARRIED LOVE**

Second Day   **OPENING OUR MINDS**

Third Day   **FUSING OUR HEARTS**

Fourth Day   **JOINING OUR WILLS**

Fifth Day   **REVEALING OUR INNERMOST SELF**

Sixth Day   **SHARING ABOUT GOD'S LOVE**

Seventh Day **EXPERIENCING A FACE TO FACE ENCOUNTER**

"Love One Another Just As I Loved You!"

Jesus of Nazareth

BECOMING ONE

The Fourth Week is the core of this book. Its main purpose is to offer each married couple an opportunity to discover the way to happiness in marriage, by having a unique experience of total unity.

Becoming one is God's Dream for each married couple. At the same time it is the innermost longing of every husband and wife. The journey toward total unity is precisely the mysterious process of happiness in marriage and family life.

Unhappiness occurs in marriage when a husband and wife realize that their lives are not meshing together, but instead are moving farther and farther apart. Then, a bitter feeling of frustration and impotence takes possession of the spouses. They come to the fatal conclusion that their longing for a happy marriage is a false illusion and an impossible dream. Why is this fatal conviction reached by so many of today's married couples?

In general, awareness of frustration and unhappiness in marriage does not happen overnight. It is the final stage of a chain of frustrations and emptiness that is rooted in a false belief that the union of the bodies themselves is the secret of marriage happiness. The union of bodies between husband and wife, according to God's Will, is a visible sign of something deeper; the union of minds, wills and souls. That is why physical union between spouses, when it is not preceded, accompanied and followed by a spiritual and internal union of minds, hearts, wills and souls, becomes a meaningless and empty sign.

The encounter of minds, hearts, wills and souls is the essence of happiness in marriage. What is the key for that internal and spiritual encounter between husband and wife to become one?

MUTUAL CONFIDING

Mutual confiding is the human way to become one. What is mutual confiding?
— A mutual opening of one's intimate life.
— An ability to share with each other the whole self.
— Faith and hope in the partner.
— A personal decision to share all with the spouse in a progressive way.
— A permanent disposition to share all the time with one's partner, despite all the internal and external difficulties.
— A habit to communicate with each other the every day, little things.
— A mutual honesty to relate to each other without masks, lies or ambiguities.

117

— A reciprocal giving and receiving without reservations.
— A deep conviction that apart from professional or confessional secrets, everything belongs to the two of them.
— A mutual simplicity and transparency of treatment.
— A mature fruit of daily communication between husband and wife.
— A precious gift of self spouses can give each other.
— A covenant or sacred commitment between the married couple and God.

How to develop mutual confiding?

- Not by demanding it, but by proposing it to each other.
- By a daily sharing of one's personal lived experiences.
- By doing things together.
- By writing "love letters" to each other. By praying together spontaneously.

TESTIMONIES

ALLAN: "I like to think of confidence in our marriage as a faith in myself, and in Laura, which allows each of us to open up our innermost selves to one another, without fear of reprisal, betrayal or ridicule, even though it exposes us to the risk all of these. If we don't have this kind of trust and confidence in our marriage and in each other, our verbal exchanges are merely a discussion of thoughts, ideas or facts at a very superficial level.

"For some of us, probably mostly us guys, exposing our fears to someone else is something we learned as kids that we shouldn't do: 'Big boys aren't afraid,' 'Big boys don't cry.' We hear it from the time we are small, and we learn to squelch our emotions and feelings, keep them inside, and never admit them to anyone, especially a female. But confidence in marriage means confidence in our spouse. If we are to grow close to each other, we have to expose our real self to our partner.

"Part of our self is our fears. When I let go of my deepest fears to Laura, I know she won't tell someone else; I know she won't laugh at me or think less of me because I am afraid. Rather she'll care more deeply for me because I am being honest with her.

"Probably the time in our lives when we most needed our mutual trust, confidence and dialogue with each other, was when Laura was diagnosed as having breast cancer. The overwhelming fear I felt at that time is almost indescribable. But the problem was, I was afraid to talk to Laura about my fears, because she was the one who, I felt, should have more reasons to be afraid than I. After all, I was healthy and she was not.

"From the beginning of this crisis, I put on a strong front and I didn't share my fears with Laura. Of course, I hadn't really faced all the fears that were inside me. But as I sat alone in the surgery waiting room during the operation, I realized that I had to quit playing a "macho game," and really face my fears and share them with Laura. I thought the problem was how do I say to Laura, "Have you faced the fact that you might die?" In reality, the problem was, "Have I faced the fact that you might die?"

"The day after Laura got out of the hospital, we were driving up the freeway and I started to tell her how afraid I was that she would die and leave me. Then we promised each other that we would talk about each fear or thought we had during the next frightening weeks. Our confidence in our honest dialogue made it possible for Laura and me to really come to grips with our real, inside feelings."

LAURA: "Dialogue, by definition, can be an exchange of ideas or an intimate communication.

For Allan and me, it means the open sharing of ourselves with each other — all our emotional, spiritual and physical feelings; the sharing of each other's joys, fears, happiness and loneliness, and the sharing of each emotional high or sadness through the total range of our personal experiences. It means a sharing of the very essence of our beings as nearly as we can verbalize or physically communicate it at any given moment in time.

Confidence can exist alone, and dialogue can exist without confidence, but each is beautifully enhanced by the other. Confidence is the ability to open one's self up and to share; and dialogue is the vehicle we can use. Confidence and dialogue together become the mutual trust that builds friendship between us.

My trust in Allan became more important to me as the weeks and months went by. As the medication and treatment began to alter my appearance, it started affecting, of all things, my ego and my self-image.

I started having thoughts like, "How can a man love a woman with an ugly, cut-up breast, with hair growing on her stomach and face, and with new muscles developing in her arms and shoulders?"

I remember once asking him, "If you die and I marry someone else, should I tell him about my unattractive breast before I go to bed with him or after?"

Each time my fears would come up, Allan would talk them through with me. His reassurance of his love, both verbally and in his actions, was the comfort I needed. I could trust him with my innermost fears, and I knew that he would never betray my trust by telling someone else, or by telling me I was being silly.

It was truly our mutual trust, our confidence and dialogue, that got Allan and me through this difficult period in our lives.

That's what confidence and dialogue is for us: the sharing of our burdens as well as joys; the sharing of our fears as well as hopes; and the sharing of our weaknesses as well as strengths."

WRITING LOVE LETTERS

When was the last time you wrote a love letter to your spouse? Why do love letters stop at the altar?

According to the experience of thousands of married couples all over the world, writing love letters to the spouse is an exciting and practical way to enhance marital communication and mutual confiding in marriage.

Sometimes, this is the best way to express one's personal lived experiences and to reach out to one's spouse in a very direct, honest, and loving style. Sometimes, writing a love letter is a nice bridge for two spouses who need to be reconciled with each other.

How do you write a love letter?

Writing a love letter is a personal affair. Below is a little outline: the fruit of couples who have shared their love letters with me.

1. KEEP YOUR SPOUSE IN YOUR MIND AND IN YOUR HEART, and reflect about what you want most to share with him/her.

2. BEGIN WITH A SPONTANEOUS ENDEARMENT: a sincere word of praise, a warm compliment, or a little good news.

3. BE HONEST AND SIMPLE by avoiding intellectual and sophisticated words or expressions.

4. BE YOURSELF by describing your personal lived experiences.

5. BE CONVERSATIONAL AND WARM by writing with loving details.

6. BE POSITIVE by underlining the encouraging and challenging points as you go along

7. BE DELICATE AND FINE by giving your painful experiences with tenderness.

8. LET your learning and caring for him/her be strongly voiced in your love letter.

9. END with an encouraging endearment.

10. KEEP your love letter with you until the right moment.

Are you ready to write love letters to your spouse? Just try it!

STRENGTHENING OUR MARRIED LOVE

RICHARD AND KRISTEN'S LOVE LETTERS

Dear Kristen,

One of the qualities which first attracted me to you was how pretty you are, especially your sparkly eyes and beautiful smile. That said to me, "There is a lively woman."

I liked you, darling, because you laughed at my jokes. I was impressed when you told me I didn't have to spend a lot of money on our first picnic, because you knew second lieutenants didn't make much money. I liked how you shared about your family and how proud you were of them.

It impressed me when your boss told me you were very honest. I agreed. I guess most of all I was impressed with your honesty, openness, courage, and willingness to do the right thing even though you ran a risk doing it. These were qualities I admired and envied, and that I wanted our kids to have. Later on I realized that I needed to develop these qualities myself, and that I could.

I married you, darling, for all these reasons and also because I was more comfortable with you than any woman I'd ever met.

Wow, I love you a lot!

Richard.

Dear Richard,

The more we share the more I realize anew what a fun person you are. Yet you are so gentle, down to earth, appreciative and godly.

You had all these qualities when we first met but you've become more and more special to me because of the tremendous growth I've seen in you over the years.

Hon, you are now even more fun loving; a better listener; more sensitive to my needs, hurts, desires and expectations; more affirming and godly. You are my very special friend.

I feel so grateful for each day I live my life with you.

I thank God for having provided you for me.

I love you so much,

Kristen.

ORIENTATION

The purpose of this First Day is to write a Love Letter to your spouse; to reveal your love to him/her.

How Do You Do It?

Write a Love Letter to your spouse to reveal your love for him/her. Express, emphasize and describe it, as best you can, after reflecting on the following questions:

- WHY DID I MARRY YOU?

- WHAT ARE THE QUALITIES THAT MOST ATTRACTED ME TO YOU?

- HOW MUCH DO I LOVE YOU?

After personally reflecting on the above questions, write your Love Letter.

OPENING OUR MINDS

DAVID AND ARLINE'S LOVE LETTERS

Dear Arline,

Tonight, I need to confide in you that I want to keep living, to continue to grow and become more of the unique person God wants me to be: more loving, more open, more willing to take risks, more accepting of myself and others, more flexible, less rigid, interested in more things, more willing to try them, assuming more responsibility for myself and what I do.

I want to go on living with you because you are beautiful, charming, godly, and sexy. With you I can be myself because you challenge me to grow. You are fun. We have great sexual relations. I can help you to grow and be more yourself because I can learn from your spunky, open, honest, loving characteristics and grow myself in this way.

My dreams about us are that I can retire in the near future and that we will continue to grow as individuals, as a couple and as a family. That we will be able to have fulfilling things as individuals and as a couple. That we can expand our ministry together. That we know God's peace and joy and love. Have a beautiful, growing relationship with our family. Keep our priorities of self, God, us, family, neighbors and ministry straight . . . Arline, you are the inspiration for all my dreams. Thank you for loving me.

I love you always,

David.

Dear David,

As you know, God is using me to love others unconditionally and that is a wonderful reason for living. When I'm rejected and admonished and can turn around and say I'm sorry for causing someone pain and ask for forgiveness, I feel grateful for the grace to love no matter what. If I can continue to give my hurt to the Lord and see the hurt in others that causes them to act the way they do, I feel excited about life.

Thank you David, for helping me to become more and deny myself or others. You're good for me. You make it easy for me to keep the Lord first because you are such a good example of a godly person. I'm blessed.

I dream that we can know more and more about how the Lord is using us as a couple to give to others. If our lives and our testimony can continue to help other married people get on the right track, my dreams for us will be realized.

I love you forever,

Arline.

ORIENTATION

Write a Love Letter to your spouse about your main dreams, thoughts, opinions, judgments, convictions, priorities, beliefs and reasons for living and loving, so you can become One Mind.

Use the following questions to reflect on:

- WHAT ARE MY MAIN REASONS FOR WANTING TO GO ON LIVING?

- WHAT ARE MY MAIN REASONS FOR WANTING TO GO ON LIVING WITH YOU?

- WHAT ARE MY DREAMS ABOUT YOU AND ME?

After personally reflecting on the previous questions, write your Love Letter.

FUSING OUR HEARTS

ED AND SALLY'S LOVE LETTERS

Dearest Sally,

One of my greatest fears is that in my weakness I will get involved with another woman. I believe this ties in with my fear of success. We are so happy and have so much sexually, and every other way, I have a need/desire to foul myself up. Also my dad's getting involved with another woman is part of it.

Father, I give this to you. Thank you, Lord, for your love, protection, grace and strength on this.

I am concerned about our (really my) drinking, especially in retirement. We do well through the week, drinking nothing, but I tend to drink too much on the weekend. Thank you, Lord, for giving me the desire and grace to drink moderately.

My joys are relaxing, getting satisfaction from doing productive, creative things 3-4 hours a day, our sexual relations, traveling, planning trips, going out to dinner, being with you, sharing, growing, being with our family, being open to God's grace to accept and deal with problems.

My expectations about you are that you will continue to be my loving wife, continue to grow and share with me, allow me to be myself while helping and challenging me to grow, be a neat, wonderful wife in retirement and in our ministry.

Sally, I love you very much, You are beautiful.
All my love,

Ed.

Dear Ed,

One of the hurts I find difficult to share with you, Ed, is my need to have you really listen to me. I need to know you care about my day and the many accomplishments and frustrations I have — not just ask to ask and let it go in one ear and out the other.

I'm unhappy when I sense you're off in another world of thought rather than asking questions about what I'm telling you.

I'm happy for the closeness we know and for the deeper love this sharing will bring. I know I can expect you to give more of you to me because of this need. I'm excited about that.

Thank you for loving me,

Sally.

ORIENTATION

The purpose of today's Love Letter is to share with your spouse your: feelings, sentiments and emotions, fears, concerns, expectations, disappointments, frustrations, impressions, joys, sorrows, griefs, happiness and unhappiness, to become one heart.

To encourage you to reflect first, and then write, here are a few suggested questions:

- WHICH ARE THOSE FEELINGS, FEARS, CONCERNS, DISAPPOINTMENTS, FRUSTRATIONS OR SORROWS, I FIND DIFFICULT TO SHARE WITH YOU?

- ACTUALLY, WHAT MAKES ME UNHAPPY AND WHAT MAKES ME HAPPY ABOUT OUR LIVES?

- WHICH ARE MY EXPECTATIONS ABOUT YOU?

JOINING OUR WILLS

LAUREN AND TYLER'S LOVE LETTERS

Dear Lauren,

The positive signs that I have decided to spend a lifetime with you are our sharing, our growing family — sons, daughters-in-law, grandchildren — our ministry, our proposed retirement.

I need to listen better to your needs and be less selfish in fulfilling them, e.g., your wanting to eat out yesterday.

My limitations include my fear of sticking my neck out, my lack of openness with you and others for fear you may criticize me, my unwillingness to be lovingly confrontive.

My possibilities are that, with God's grace, I will — and am — being more open, more loving, more honest, more lovingly confrontive. As it gets more painful not to change, I am sticking my neck out, seeing myself as more important than the job. This scares me. I feel guilty and afraid.

With God's help and a lovingly honest wife — Miss Lauren — I will spend the rest of my life being open, honest, loving — and exposing this attitude as ungodly and unrealistic.

I love you, hon,

Tyler.

Dear Tyler,

My greatest yearning is to grow closer to the Lord each day. Since my life with you makes this easier to do, I am convinced of needing you always, to help me accomplish my dream. You are nice!

I need to accept the fact that shampooing your hair is such a big deal for you. Let's talk about this more so I can better understand what makes you tick. I love you.

I feel sad about not feeling in charge of the money I have in the bank, hon. Going halfsies with you is fun, and I enjoy helping with trips and presents, but I'm frustrated with taking out more than I'm able to put in. Periodically this happens — like splitting the money for the last two trips. Maybe I should try to save more each week but I hate scrimping and doing without — which I think I'd have to do. I'd like your insights to help me feel better about money.

Thanks for being my friend,

Lauren.

ORIENTATION

Today, your Love Letter could be about: your personal wants, desires, attitudes, choices, resolutions and decisions, goals, likes and dislikes, commitments, attempts and efforts to become One Will.

To encourage you to reflect first, and then write, here are a few suggested questions:

- WHAT ARE MY OWN PERSONAL WANTS, DESIRES, ATTITUDES, CHOICES, RESOLUTIONS AND DECISIONS, GOALS, LIKES AND DISLIKES, COMMITMENTS, ATTEMPTS OR EFFORTS I NEED TO SHARE WITH YOU SO YOU WILL BE ABLE TO HELP ME?

- WHAT DO I HONESTLY NEED TO ACCEPT ABOUT YOU THAT I HAVE NOT ACCEPTED YET?

- WHAT ARE THE POSITIVE SIGNS WHICH SHOW THAT I HAVE CHOSEN YOU FOR A LIFETIME?

REVEALING OUR INNERMOST SELF

VIRGINIA'S TESTIMONY

Jesus' statement, "The truth will set you free" has special meaning for Max and me because it saved our marriage from inner death. When Max and I got married, we were idealistic 'sixties types' who really believed that if we remained completely honest with each other, our friendship and our love would always stay alive. The true testimony of our idealism came later on, when our physical fidelity was challenged.

Max's 'indiscretion' came early in our marriage: something more than flirtation and less than a full-fledged affair. He was full of guilt, and torn up inside. After agonizing about whether or not to share the truth with me, Max decided to admit the mistake that he would much rather have kept secret. About seven years later, I had a brief affair and confessed it to him too.

When I had thoughts like 'What he doesn't know won't hurt him,' or 'He won't be able to take the hurt,' I was belittling Max. Deep in my heart I had the confidence that Max was a real adult — a real man — and he could deal with the truth as long as I spoke with love. I had to have a 'heap of faith' that our love would be strong handle confrontation.

To keep things secret from each other would have meant a lifetime of deception upon deception, a constant watching over our words to make sure we didn't let the wrong thing 'slip'. It's true that we weave a tangled web when first we begin to deceive. If I had allowed Max to believe a lie, my thoughts and my words could never be free. I'd always be self-censoring. I'd always feel on guard. My naturalness and spontaneity would suffer, and my guilt feelings would weigh me down. Love would have become more burden than joy.

When Max told me the truth, I was hurt and angry. When I told him the truth, he was hurt and angry. But after the truth was out in the open, we could yell and argue and cry and lie quietly and talk for hours. We could let all our feelings out. Often a truth-crisis like this exposes things we didn't even know were locked inside us. So we gain self-revelation and deeper self-knowledge . . . as well as a closer bond with our mate.

Later, Max and I learned through Marriage Encounter that our long talks had a fancy name: dialogue. Without truth there is no dialogue. Without truth, there is no intimacy. With truth — no matter how much it hurts sometimes — we have potential to grow closer to each other than ever before. Closer than words can say and closer than sex can express. It is the closeness of the spirit.

ORIENTATION

For revealing the most intimate part of your real self to your spouse — through your Love Letter — you will have to freely and, as a friend, confide in him/her some of your personal: troubles, struggles, temptations, defeats, victories, doubts, internal sufferings and deep consolations, little or big secrets, so you will be able to let your spouse enter into the very center of yourself to become One Soul.

The following questions are just for your inspiration.

- WHAT KIND OF SELF-REVELATION OR SELF-DISCOVERY WOULD I LIKE TO SHARE WITH YOU?

- WHEN I AM MOST DISCOURAGED, WHAT GETS ME UP TO RETURN TO THE STRUGGLE?

- WHAT WOULD I LIKE TO KNOW MOST ABOUT YOUR INNER SELF?

Reflect, and afterwards write your Love Letter.

SHARING ABOUT GOD'S LOVE

TWO LOVE LETTERS TO GOD

Dear God,

Thank you for being my Savior, for dying for me, for being so powerful, loving, and for being my best friend. Thank you for forgiving me, for choosing me, for the desire you put in me to live my life as you lived yours. Thank you for sending me Jane and our beautiful family.

Thank you for healing our marriage wounds and giving us your spirit of reconciliation and peace.

Thank you also, Lord, for healing my problem of getting an erection. You really are the greatest!

Thank you for helping us to continue to be open and loving, to communicate, to grow as individuals — closer to you and to each other.

I love you, Lord.

Jim.

Dear Heavenly Father,

This is neat, writing to you, because I don't do it often enough. You're so good to me — you chose me and called me to be your own. You forgive my sins because you love me so much. You've made my life so fulfilling with Him.

You're my Lord, my Saviour, my King, my everything. Oh, I'm so grateful to you for being so good to me. You constantly love and affirm me; you show me how you're using me.

You're quite a model for me to live by. All I need do is reflect on your love for me and I'll be able to fulfill your will for me — "Love one another as I loved you." If Jim and I do this as a couple, I know you'll be thrilled with our lives here on earth.

Help us, Lord to be all you want us to be.

Lord God, teach me every day to be less judgmental of others. Show me how small my world is so I can get a greater glimpse of the joy you want for me.

And most of all, never let me part from you.

Your loving daughter,

Anne.

ORIENTATION

The purpose of this Sixth Day is very special.

Both of you are invited to write a personal Love Letter to GOD.

How do you do it?

Simply by becoming aware of God's presence and action in your personal life:

His Calls. His Gifts. His Inspirations. His Lights.

His Power. His Merciful Compassion. His Healing.

His Messages. His Friendship. His Love.

Just write to Him, after reflecting about these three questions:

- GOD, WHO ARE YOU FOR ME?

- HOW DO I FEEL YOUR LOVE?

- LORD, WHAT DO I HAVE TO THANK YOU FOR THE MOST?

EXPERIENCING A
FACE TO FACE ENCOUNTER

TESTIMONIES

- "After 11 years of marriage I found it difficult to realize that we did not share our total self yet, but our "love letters" were very meaningful experiences. This week we have had the chance to evaluate ourselves in areas we never did before and we feel like we are starting a new marriage life."—Ellen.

- "Really this week has been the best and also the most difficult for me. I shared some things about my personal life with her for the first time, which I always held back because I thought they were too negative or too personal. It was painful for both of us but we definitely grew as a result. I still had a bundle of hurt inside when we went to bed but her love and affection has increased my confidence to be open. During our great dialogue I discovered the deepness of her love for me. She shared with me things like her need for mutual signs of affection and more frequent sex, and the need to communicate the every-day happiness and unhappiness. So now I feel warm, loving and optimistic about our future."—Burt.

- "What I liked the most was our total and mutual confidence in our Love Letters because it goes to the essence of our marriage. Really with God's help we were able to begin a new way of life in our relationship."—Patricia.

- "Before this week I had difficulty in sharing my true 'self' for fear of being laughed at or hurt. But this week we have shared meaningful experiences I never mentioned before. It was more difficult than what we had been doing before. It was total and deep communication."—Cary.

- "It resulted in one of the best dialogues that Mary and I have had. We can see how much deeper our relationship can grow if we can communicate these lived experiences to each other. Through the 'love letters' I felt a lot better knowing that she not only loves me, but listens to me and appreciates me, too. I've found it refreshing and encouraging."—Teddy.

- "The past few days have brought us to the present, the right now which we can share. It has reminded us of where we were, and reinforced where we want to go. It has been a marvelous journey, full of sorrow and joy, full of giving and receiving ourselves. Thank you for calling us to this experience."—Laura.

- "The past few days have brought us to the present, the right now which we can share. It has reminded us of where we were, and reinforced where we want to go. It has been a marvelous journey, full of sorrow and joy, full of giving and receiving ourselves. Thank you for calling us to this experience."—Laura.

- "After hours of dialogues we have shared our closeness and joy much more intensely than ever before. Now we have just opened the door for a new and total communication in our marriage."—Krista.

ORIENTATION

After both of you have written your Love Letters, it is time to get together to exchange them with each other.

To make this a special time, something unique and unforgettable, it would be good for you to sit a couple of hours in your favorite spot, to share and discuss your Love Letters in a loving and peaceful attitude of reaching out and mutual confiding.

SUGGESTED PROCEDURE

- You could start by facing each other with tenderness and affection — caring, touching, kissing, hugging.

- You could light a candle and make a short prayer to invite the Lord to your sharing.

- Then, you could exchange your Love Letters and read them two times: first with your head, and afterwards with your heart.

- When both of you have finished reading all your spouse's Love Letters, you could begin to make your personal comments by,

— BEING POSITIVE — avoiding all kinds of negative comments.

— SHOWING GRATITUDE, for those points of your spouse's Love Letters that have encouraged you the most.

— ASKING AND GIVING FORGIVENESS for whatever mistake or fault you are becoming aware of through your reading.

— AFFIRMING AND ENCOURAGING each other for whatever your spouse needs to be affirmed, stimulated or supported.

— EMPHASIZING the special messages that are emerging from each other.

— MAKING some kind of covenant or commitment to keep the fire of conjugal love and communication alive and growing.

Are We
Spiraling
Out?

Fifth Week

ARE WE SPIRALING OUT?

First Day   **GETTING ALONG WITH OUR CHILDREN**

Second Day   **ENRICHING OUR FAMILY LIFE**

Third Day   **BEING AN OPEN FAMILY**

Fourth Day   **TAKING CARE OF OUR RELATIVES**

Fifth Day   **MAKING FRIENDS AS A FAMILY**

Sixth Day   **APPROACHING OUR NEIGHBORS**

Seventh Day   **REACHING OUT TO THE POOR AND NEEDY**

"Love does not consist in gazing at each other, but in looking together in the same direction."

A. De Saint-Exupery

Any time husband and wife experience a deep interpersonal encounter, they are tempted afterwards to keep their intimacy and closeness for themselves only, by building a circle around them, and excluding from their love circle the rest of the world. This way they create a universe "just for the two of us."

This selfish and proud attitude is against God's Vision, and consequently, against the spouses themselves. God created man and woman, not to die in a vicious circle of selfish love, but to give meaning, life and love to the universe. In fact, He created marriage "to His image and likeness," and God is not a circle. He is the spiraling foundation of Life and Love. That is why after He created them, as the Bible says, "God blessed them, saying to them, 'Be fruitful, multiply, fill the earth and conquer it'. "

On the other hand, love is an expensive energy. It only grows to the extent that it is shared. Conjugal love, as a living spiral of life and love, is like a fire. It must be spread or it will be extinguished. Therefore, it is very important for you, as a married couple, to consider how you can share your energy of conjugal life and love with others.

The quest for happiness in marriage demands that you expand your vision and perspective beyond your marital relationships. The good news is two-fold: you are challenged by today's society to stop being a selfish and isolated married couple. And you are called by the Creator to depart from your conjugal and family love, and go towards the universal love . . .

In fact, as Saint-Exupery writes: "Love does not consist in gazing at each other, but in looking together in the same direction."

You, as a married couple, have been born to become a loving spiral of love.

TESTIMONIES

- "This Week helped us to focus on an area that is vital and really should be explored in real depth. We have observed that for many couples, including ourselves, children are 'taboo.' Often, we are reluctant to bring up the subject to avoid friction in our marriage. We realize that frequently we are at opposite ends of the pole when it comes to children."

- "I have realized that our children come before friends and relatives. The difficult point was admitting to ourselves all of the mistakes of the past with our children."

- "I have discovered that we must develop a closer relationship with our children and not be complacent about the way we are now. I never thought of asking forgiveness from my children for my mistakes, yet I expect it from them."

- "The most effective part of this Week has been the sharing with the children. It was very easy for us to come in touch with the areas of 'our important mistakes' with regard to them and to prepare a wonderful reconciliation: not spending enough time with them; not listening closely enough; lack of presence and affection, not affirming and praising them enough; inconsistency; taking out our trauma about outside situations on them . . .

  When we talked with our three children — 7, 6 and 5 years old — they were so simple and open. We need to be with them so much more."

- "This Week gave us the wonderful opportunity to experience something we had wanted to do for months but did not have the courage. The reconciliation with our children — 11, 15 and 19 years old — as an essential part of this program, has been the 'turning point' and was the beginning of a new style of life."

- "I liked this Week because it gave us a chance to include our 10-year-old son in our time together. He really appreciated our openness with him, and he was happy to be able to help us regarding our treatment of him. He appreciated our asking his forgiveness for the first time."

- "The reconciliation with our children was meaningful to us. The Lord pointed out through them that we were not listening. We were hearing their requests, which amounted to words, but we were not hearing the music — feelings, frustrations, needs, desires, loneliness, anger, jealousy, lack of self-esteem, dissatisfaction with our expression of love, and toleration."

- "We are learning that God speaks to us through our children, if we listen to them."

The
First Day

GETTING ALONG WITH OUR CHILDREN

Your children. They are the number one priority, after your marital relationship. They come before your own social and career ambitions. They are not your possession, but God's gift on loan to you. We are talking about parental love. What are the basic ingredients? How do you practice it?

BEING IN PERSONAL AND DIRECT TOUCH WITH EACH ONE, by attending and listening to each one actively. It means spending quality time and one's best energies with each one of them.

RESPECTING THEM by not making decisions about their future without consulting them, but giving them the opportunity to make their own choices.

ACCEPTING THEM AS THEY REALLY ARE. Especially when they become teenagers, but before, too. When negative attitudes are prevalent in the home, children tend to have low self-esteem, resulting in poor relationships and more problems, like drugs, alcohol, premarital sex, runaways, delinquency, crime and suicide.

CONFIDING AND TRUSTING THEM, always, but especially when they are growing up. Experience shows that the quality of their responsibility is proportional to the quality of your trust and confidence. You cannot demand trust and confidence; you have to earn and deserve it.

RECOGNIZING AND AFFIRMING THEM ALL, but especially the little ones. On your loving appreciation is rooted his/her healthy self-esteem and future behavior in life.

SHARING OPENLY WITH THEM: your strong points and your weak ones; your needs and values; your concerns; your expectations; your time; your energies; your talents; your dreams and hopes.

RECONCILING WITH THEM, by asking their forgiveness for your misunderstandings, faults and mistakes; by healing them with the oil of your humility, honesty, sincerity and love.

CARING FOR THEM, with tenderness, as the pupil of your eye.

PLAYING WITH AND ENJOYING THEM, having a good time together. Fun is the hook for togetherness.

ASKING THEM FOR THEIR HELP AND ENCOURAGE-MENT. Sometimes, the key for improving your personal relationship with your son or daughter, could be by receiving from him/her something that he/she has and you don't. Give your children the opportunity of giving.

PRAYING TOGETHER, after dialoguing, of course! Without the loving power of God, getting along will be an impossible dream.

Suggested Action

WRITING LOVE LETTERS TO YOUR SONS AND DAUGHTERS

The purpose of these Love Letters is to express in the best way you can, your personal appreciation, respect, understanding, confidence, acceptance, support and love, to each one of your sons and daughters, in accordance with their age, needs, talents and particular expectations.

To inspire you for a personal reflection before writing, here are a couple of questions:

1. WHAT DO I LIKE MOST IN EACH ONE OF MY CHILDREN?

2. SO FAR, WHAT HAVE BEEN MY PERSONAL MISTAKES AND FAULTS REGARDING EACH ONE OF MY SONS AND DAUGHTERS?

3. FOR WHAT, IN PARTICULAR, DO I NEED THEIR UNDERSTANDING, HELP, SUPPORT AND ENCOURAGEMENT?

Once you have reflected on the previous points, you will be able to write your Love Letter to your Sons and Daughters.

Afterwards, before a conjugal exchange, you can deliver them at the best opportunity and time.

The
Second Day

ENRICHING OUR FAMILY LIFE

Like a caterpillar is destined by its nature to be transformed into a wonderful butterfly, a married couple has been created by God to become a healthy, strong and happy family. What is a happy family? What makes a family become strong and healthy? How can you become one?

According to the encouraging testimony of happy families all over, the keys or basic elements are:

COMMUNION MENTALITY. They give top priority to their family group over jobs, careers, extra income, problems at work and social life. They feel community and work for communion and unity through a balanced interdependence among them and by avoiding independence and dominion.

DETERMINATION AND COURAGE. They usually deal with crises constructively by seeing something positive in every situation, no matter how bad, and they focus on the positive aspect by joining together, as a family, to face the crisis head on. And if they need help, they ask for it.

PERSON-TO-PERSON-COMMUNICATION. They share personally and honestly with each other: their thoughts, feelings, judgements, attitudes, concerns, needs, aspirations, choices and decisions. They listen to each other with deep respect. They dedicate quality time for periodical family dialogues. They reconcile with each other whenever they need it.

MUTUAL NOURISHMENT AND SUPPORT. They love each other not for what they have or do, but for what they are. They show appreciation and tenderness for each other. They notice and praise the positive qualities and talents in each one of the family members. They help each other to become aware of who each one is, and make each other feel good about themselves.

TOGETHERNESS. They do a lot of things together, and really enjoy each other, and spend a great deal of time together, by structuring their lives so that they can be together. When life outside gets too hectic, they sit down and list their activities, then, cut some to free up time for family togetherness. . . They have a sense of humor. They sing. They play and have fun together.

143

FAMILY PRAYER. They accept God as a Supreme Ruler and Lord of their home life. They share spiritual values and religious experiences. They worship God together. They listen to Him and speak to Him with respect and confidence. They ask His forgiveness and for family peace. They give thanks to Him daily.

Suggested Action

CELEBRATING AROUND OUR TABLE

Families everywhere celebrate at their dinner table. It is a clear sign of happiness and a powerful means to increase and improve family life. Happy families don't just happen! They work at it, and they work at it regularly. How do they celebrate?

They follow regular traditions, rituals and customs. They celebrate special days like holidays, birthdays, anniversaries and feasts, as a family.

Family celebrations are important to create close ties and bonds. Sometimes, it only takes one good family experience to start a tradition, and to carry it over into the next generation or longer.

When was your last family celebration? When is the next celebration around your table going to be?

Just choose one of the following list and . . . celebrate your family love!

- A BIRTHDAY — look on the Calendar!
- AN ANNIVERSARY: Wedding, Baptism . . .
- NAME'S DAY.
- FATHER'S DAY.
- MOTHER'S DAY.
- CHILDREN'S DAY.
- WEDDING DAY.
- FAMILY DAY.
- GRANDPARENTS' DAY.
- FRIENDS' DAY
- GRADUATION DAY
- RECONCILIATION DAY
- PATRIOTIC DAY.
- RELIGIOUS DAY.
- THANKSGIVING DAY.
- CHRISTMAS DAY.
- EASTER or PASSOVER DAY.
- NEW YEAR or HANUKKAH DAY.
- VALENTINE'S DAY.

144

BEING AN OPEN FAMILY

Families go on and on, and move and move, and change and change.

Openness is another essential dimension of happiness in the family. It is the test of its genuine and profound unity. Without openness, families die of suffocation; their happiness is superficial. Family openness is rooted in its very nature. The inner call to become a family is the call to build an open and dynamic community, creator of life and of interpersonal relations.

Self-centered families are the denial of family itself. The lack of openness is a cancerous evil that destroys a family slowly. On the other hand, the main traits of family openness are: altruism, generosity, simplicity, solidarity, commitment, creativity, hospitality, spirit of service, cheerfulness, kindness, involvement, joy and peace.

How Can You Become An Open Family?

1. WORKING FOR UNITY AND COMMUNION inside of one's own family. This is the departing point for true openness. Unity and communion between husband and wife, parents and children, brothers and sisters, family and God.

    Without this internal and intimate harmony, all attempt for openness will damage family members and the family itself. It also will be negative testimony in the community.

2. EDUCATING FOR LOVE. This is the key for genuine openness. In other words, being aware: that persons are more important than things, and to be there for others is more important than to have or to do.

    Also discovering the dignity, rights and values of everybody and avoiding dominating, manipulating, and discriminating. Instead, to serve, to cooperate and to be involved. Briefly: educating to give and share rather than to get.

145

3. PRACTICING HOSPITALITY. This is the best expression of an open family. Happy families are spontaneously hospitable. Hospitality is what makes a house become a home. You will practice hospitality if you make your house a home for everybody, by welcoming them so they feel comfortable, safe and loved. Home is the place where love abides and you share it with everybody.

Home is not just a place, it is more than that, it is a loving attitude of welcoming people as they are. Actually, your home is where your heart is.

Suggested Action

MAKING A FAMILY AGREEMENT

Being an open family is not a magic trick. All the members of the family, as a unit, have to work towards it.

The purpose of your next Family Dialogue could be to create a simple, but specific Family Agreement on family openness.

Before you get together to share, it would be good for each member of the family to have a personal time to reflect and to answer the following questions:

1. ARE WE A UNITED FAMILY?

2. WHICH ARE THE POSITIVE SIGNS OF UNITY AND COMMUNION IN OUR FAMILY?

3. ARE WE AN OPEN FAMILY?

4. ARE WE HOSPITABLE?

5. HOW DO WE ACTUALLY PRACTICE HOSPITALITY?

6. HOW COULD WE IMPROVE OUR OPENNESS?

When everybody is ready, get together to share your personal answers to the previous questions, so you will be able to formulate your Family Agreement about openness and hospitality.

TAKING CARE OF OUR RELATIVES

Family openness has to be experienced to grow like a spiral of life and love: from inside to outside.

1. GRANDPARENTS
They are number one and an essential part of our families.

In the past, people lived in extended families. That means that grandparents regularly lived with their sons and daughters, grandsons and granddaughters. Today, the so-called nuclear or conjugal families have reduced their membership. Most grandparents do not live with their children anymore. They live by themselves, or are pushed aside or abandoned.

What is happening with the Fourth Commandment of God's Law?

2. UNCLES AND AUNTS
They are our parents's brothers and sisters. They live in their own homes with their sons and daughters. They are another nuclear family. Maybe isolated, separated or divorced.

What happened to our brotherly love?

3. NEPHEWS AND NIECES
They are our brother's and sisters's sons and daughters, and cousins of our children. Perhaps, they are our godchildren too, and so, we are more linked to them. Today, many of them are searching for their identity: some have problems with their parents; are alcoholic or drug addicts, have a poor self-esteem; are runaways; are being abused; are strongly involved in sexual experiences; are delinquents; are being tempted to commit suicide; maybe are orphans or thirsty for God . . .

What actually is happening to each one of them?

4. IN-LAWS
They really are important to us because they are blood of our beloved spouses. In fact, what are their values, their problems and their needs?

Suggested Action

REVIVING OUR FAMILY TREE

Families, like trees, are planted. They are born. They grow. And they die. But families are more than trees. They can be reborn.

Today, most families are unaware of their Family Tree. For many, their family tree is dying or is already dead. Why? Because the contact with their roots is broken. They try to live without a personal relationship with their relatives. Relationships are family blood. They are the key to revive the divine energy of love that is hidden within each ordinary family.

Therefore, if you want to revive your Family Tree, get together, and review your interpersonal relationships with your relatives, beginning with the grandparents.

But first, it would be good if each member of your family spent some time on their own, to reflect and to write about the following questions:

1. ARE WE TAKING CARE OF OUR RELATIVES, ESPECIALLY THE OLDEST ONES?

2. AMONG OUR RELATIVES, WHICH ONES NEED MORE OF OUR ATTENTION AND OUR INTENSIVE CARE?

3. WHAT COULD OR SHOULD WE DO, AS A FAMILY, TO HELP THEM EFFECTIVELY?

The
Fifth Day

MAKING FRIENDS AS A FAMILY

True friendship is one of the most positive and rewarding human values. Friends are a treasure. Open families have many good friends to love and to be loved by. The unconscious tendency of married couples and families to turn inward, is one of the major threats to friendship.

Most people when they get married, lose their friendship or stop developing it. They begin to depend more on each other, and they spend less time with their friends. Some married couples usually think of their friends and their families as totally separated. Others, when they marry, try to incorporate their personal friends into their new life.

In fact, friends are compatible with marriage and family life if they do not interfere or put obstacles in the way of married people and their families; on the contrary, if friends are incorporated into marriage and family life, then they will fortify and open them.

On the other hand, if your family has too few, or unhealthy, friends, your children will have to face the task of building new patterns of relating to others. These patterns will enable them to select friends who can meet their needs.

If friends are an integral part of your marriage and family life, it will help your children to grow up naturally and form creative friendships on their own. They will learn by observing your relationship with your friends. They have an astonishing capacity for imitation.

Moreover, it is important to realize that you and your children may frequently have conflict about their friends and their peer group. Then if you, with an authoritarian attitude, actively attempt to inhibit your children's friendships — by not giving them enough room to be by themselves, to have opinions, to follow their own interests and make their own mistakes; if you do not really trust their choice of friends, they will react with rebellion and violence. Or what is worse, and like a dramatic expression of their violent rebellion, they will become alcoholics, drug addicts, runaways, delinquents and probably will try to commit suicide.

Therefore, having friends inside and outside of your family is an important and transcendental goal to achieve, in the process of becoming a united and open family.

INVITING FRIENDS TO OUR HOME

There are different types or levels of friendship, according to the different needs they fulfill or the kind of intimacy they provide:

- FRIENDS TO TALK TO.
- FRIENDS TO WORK WITH.
- FRIENDS TO HAVE FUN WITH.
- FRIENDS TO SHARE WITH.
- FRIENDS TO COUNT ON.
- FRIENDS TO COMPLETELY TRUST IN.

In a family, there are various dimensions of friendship:
A. PERSONAL FRIENDS.
B. COUPLE'S FRIENDS.
C. FAMILY FRIENDS.

Also, our friends can be: individuals, couples and families.

PERSONAL REFLECTION

1. DO WE HAVE ANY CONFLICT WITH OUR PERSONAL FRIENDS?

2. DO WE HAVE FAMILY FRIENDS?

3. WHO ARE THEY?

4. WHAT LEVEL OF FRIENDSHIP DO WE HAVE WITH EACH ONE OF THEM?

5. WHEN COULD WE HAVE A CELEBRATION AT OUR HOME WITH OUR FRIENDS?

FAMILY SHARING

After reflecting and writing individually on these questions, you could gather together to share with each other, and this way, prepare a home celebration with your friends.

The
Sixth Day

APPROACHING OUR NEIGHBORS

What has happened to us and to our families that we have become afraid of our neighbors? The Golden Rule: "Love your neighbor as you love yourself," has been forgotten, or almost lost, in today's so called neighborhoods.

Love of neighbor is a most basic prerequisite of being a person, i.e., to have love for the other. But if the concept of person is reduced to a social function, or is absorbed into a materialistic or consumaristic idea, then love of neighbor misses a considerable part of its meaning, and loses its intensive force of attraction. This is precisely what is happening in our society.

Love of neighbor facilitates friendship and introduces it. Love of neighbor truly empathizes with all men and women, and makes life easier for others as well as for ourselves.

Actually, love of neighbor is grounded in God's love for all men and women. Consequently, in loving our neighbor we reproduce in ourselves the behavior of God. Genuine love of neighbor cannot be separated from God's love.

All of us understand the significance of the Golden Rule, because we understand the practical meaning of being loved — accepted — by someone. Therefore, one of the ways of going against ourselves is by moving against another, by not loving or accepting our neighbor. To love God and reject our neighbor, at the same time, is a contradiction. Yet sometimes we think we have grounds for such rejection.

Anyway, it would be wise to make a distinction about what we're rejecting. Is it for who a person is, or for what the same human being has — language, culture, color, beliefs. The second is possible, the first is not, unless we have been blinded. Where this is the case, then, we would be in need of correcting our mental image for it is defective.

Genuine love of neighbors produces joy and peace. That's why when families are open to their neighbors, they become happy.

151

ENFORCING LOVE'S GOLDEN RULE

Love's Golden Rule is not something to think about, but something to experience by approaching our neighbors with an open heart.

How Do You Do It As A Family?

Here is a list of suggested practical ways for your personal reflection and your family sharing:

- Have a "pot-luck" dinner with some neighbors, just for fun.
- Invite a single-parent family to join you for a picnic.
- Plan a neighborhood "cook out."

- Share a stew with another family.
- Take someone a casserole supper.
- Invite a new family for brunch.

- After church, invite another family for milk, coffee and donuts
- Clean up the neighborhood with your friends.
- Take a surprise dinner to someone who is pregnant.

- Be a substitute family: take a neighbor's child for a family treat.
- Invite someone to dinner who usually is alone.
- Open your home for a weekend to someone who needs love.

- Surprise your neighbor with a home-made gift.
- Do something kind for a widow or widower.
- Help an elderly or sick neighbor with some yard work.

- Run some errands for a neighbor in need.
- Offer to keep a young couple's children for the day.
- Baby-sit for a young mother for free.

- Wash an elderly person's car for free.
- Spend some time with someone with a chronic fatal illness.
- Invite some of your neighbors for a family celebration.

- Have a prayer group in your home.

REACHING OUT TO THE
POOR AND NEEDY

Truly happy families are naturally open, not only to family members, relatives, friends and neighbors, but everybody — especially the poor and needy. Anytime that one of the members of the family is aware of any kind of need, injustice, violence, hunger, poverty, unemployment, discrimination, drugs, suffering or misery, they call for a family meeting, to see what they could, or should, do on each case.

Open families are bridges for the poor and needy so they may be able to pass from injustice and violence to justice and peace. They make special efforts to seek native Americans, Blacks, Hispanics and Asians as well. Happy families are challenged to model their life on the values of peace, justice, truth, freedom and love. Happy families are called by God to offer everywhere a witness of generous and unselfish dedication to justice and peace.

How do you do it?

1. BEING POOR WITH THE POOR, by choosing a simple standard of life. Genuine family life is an experience of sharing and communion. Happy families who are spiritually rich need to simplify their family life and spend less. They could opt for a style of poverty within their own family. Sometimes, this involves making dramatic choices, saying "no" to certain consumer goods, and thus be poor with the poor.

2. BEING A CARING FAMILY FOR HURTING FAMILIES. Families often go through great suffering, pain and anxieties. Often they suffer in silence. These people are: single families — separated and divorced, widows and widowers, orphans, abandoned mothers or fathers. Also migrants, homeless, hungry, unemployed, handicapped and terminally sick; families of those in prison, etc. All those families need caring families, who assist them and who also take more incisive action on public opinion, so the deep causes of their suffering may be eliminated as far as possible, and people will be able to help themselves.

3. SUPPORTING DRUG SUFFERING FAMILIES. Drugs and alcohol scare today's families whose sons and daughters are exposed to a culture of drugs. Parents, if they are not involved themselves with drugs, are often helpless and hopeless when the problem hits their children. They also lack adequate information and education. They need support from other families. Families helping families, that is the key.

4. BEING A PEACEMAKER FAMILY. You could do it, as a family, in four ways:
   A. Overcoming selfishness, and treating everybody with respect.
   B. Avoiding dishonesty and lies, inside and outside your home.
   C. Being at peace with God, individually and as a family
   D. Showing true esteem for people. They are human beings.

Suggested Action

ACTING FOR JUSTICE AND PEACE, AS A FAMILY

In today's society, there are many possibilities for Family Action.

Each family has to find their own way of practicing justice and peace, as a unit, knowing that what is appropriate for one family, could be inappropriate for another family; and what is good for one family at this time, may not be good for the same family at another time.

Each family has to decide, through a periodical family reflection and sharing, what their own step should be in each moment of their history.

You also have to learn the necessity of taking one step at a time and always believing that every step counts.

To give you a helping hand, here are a couple of questions, for your personal reflection and family sharing.

1. ARE WE A POOR OR A RICH FAMILY?
    Please, specify the positive and negative signs of poverty or richness in your family.

2. HOW COULD WE BECOME A LOVING AND CARING FAMILY FOR A POOR, HURTING OR DRUG-SUFFERING FAMILY?
    You first must find those families near you, and see what their problem or need is, and its causes. Afterwards, together, find the right solutions.

3. ACTUALLY, HOW AND WHERE CAN WE BECOME A PEACEMAKING FAMILY.
    Do not forget that true peace and justice start inside each one of us and within our own home.

Appendix

Growing More Every Day

THE "DAILY LOVE SIGNS"
COMMITMENT

Love isn't just something you feel. Love is something you do. One of the things you can do to keep your love alive, well and growing is to practice daily little signs of love.

During the weekdays, you do not have enough time to have a nice dialogue with your spouse, but certainly you have other ways to communicate with him/her without needing a great deal of time. It doesn't take too much time to have a sign of love during the day. You only need love to express it and to make it visible and tangible.

Love's signs are little details of appreciation, affirmation and affection to your spouse.

Love's signs are a revelation about the energy of love that lies within you.

Love's signs belong to the rituals of love.

Love's signs are a living testimony of your married love.

Love's signs are sacramental. They are symbols of something beyond yourself.

How Can You Find Your Daily
Sign Of Love?

You can create your daily sign of love by asking yourselves this simple question:

IN WHICH CONCRETE WAY
WILL I SHOW MY
AFFECTION AND APPRECIATION
TO MY SPOUSE TODAY?

Following is a list of suggested signs of love for your inspiration. When you have difficulty thinking of one by yourself, you can choose one of these.

LITTLE THINGS HUSBANDS AND
WIVES CAN DO FOR EACH OTHER

- A kiss or hug: in the morning, when you come home, or just because you love each other.
- Allowing your spouse an extra hour of sleep on a weekend morning.
- Having breakfast together.
- A loving phone call: from work, or when you are out of town.
- Flowers for no reason at all.
- Smiling. A special smile with your eyes.
- Touching and holding each other.
- Surprising your spouse some way or with a little gift.
- Sending a love message at your spouse's work.
- Taking each other to lunch during the week.
- Taking time off to accompany him/her for something special.
- Helping him/her in some thing he/she needs.
- Doing something together: playing, traveling, praying, etc.
- Sacrificing something personal to please your spouse.
- Calling when you'll be late.
- Telling him/her words of praise and adoration.
- Doing shopping on the way home.
- Taking care of the problems in the house.
- Doing an equal share of the housework: washing dishes, cleaning house, cooking, etc.
- Arranging for a special night: taking him/her out to dinner.
- A warm conversation after dinner.
- Asking and giving forgiveness for something.
- Giving him/her support for his/her particular decision.
- Making time each day to listen to each other.
- Meeting him/her at the door when he/she arrives home.
- Giving your spouse time to read the paper in the evening.
- Trying to share with each other when one is withdrawn.
- Not taking him/her for granted.
- A love note in the mirror for him/her to see in the morning.
- A love letter mailed to his/her office or work.
- Taking some pressure off him/her when he/she is over-commited or hassled.
- Being sweet and kind when he/she isn't.
- Sacrificing something special or personal to please him/her.
- Cooking his/her favorite foods.

- Inviting your spouse after dinner to sit in your backyard, near your fireplace or to take a walk to share your day.
- Giving him/her time to relax and unwind after work when you want his/her time and attention.
- Listening to him/her share his/her day.
- Doing the chores you don't like to do.
- Helping him/her in something he/she needs.
- Confiding something to him/her.
- Massaging his/her shoulders after a rough day.
- Stopping yourself from telling him/her all your problems the minute he/she comes home from work.
- Not going to sleep mad at each other.

MARRIAGE ENRICHMENT PROGRAMS

What Does "Marriage Enrichment" Mean?

Do you know a gardener or farmer who doesn't annually do something to add greater value or significance to the soil for the benefit of his crops? Why should married couples do less for the benefit of their marriage and family? Marriage Enrichment means making a marriage relationship much more deep and satisfying, and enabling couples to develop skills so they can meet trouble head-on and resolve it.

In general, there is no open resistance to Marriage Enrichment programs and the need for them. The resistance is more subtle. The value is ignored. Most couples approach Marriage Enrichment with the attitude, "It's O.K. for those who need it, but we don't have any real problems."

In fact, what most fail to understand is that Marriage Enrichment is **not** for couples with serious problems. That's when a counselor is needed.

The real cop-out in the subtle resistance to "enrichment" by anyone is that none of us is immune to the tensions of life. We could all be much better at how we handle crisis, conflicts, difficulties, problems and challenges. This is true about any situation where we work or live in a relationship with another. No couple can possibly be immune from material tensions, and every couple could improve the way they handle tensions and challenges in their lives.

So, why not take advantage of the marriage enrichment programs and resources presently available?

Actually, you, as a married couple, need the support and encouragement of other married couples attending such programs. You need to know how to enrich your lives. To give you a helping-hand in your quest for marriage enrichment, following you will find a few programs and resources which are available.

CHRISTIAN FAMILY MOVEMENT

Dr. James Johnson, a sociologist at the University of Nebraska, indicates in a survey that Christian Family Movement couples are dedicated to improving their marriage and family life. They experience a high degree of happiness in these relationships.

What Is Christian Family Movement?

- The CFM is a lay movement of married couples and families who:
  — Have decided to be happier and work for sharing their happiness with other couples and families.
  — Are interested in everything related to marriage, family and community.
  — Seek a positive answer to the crises in today's world.

- The CFM is comprised of small groups of five to seven married couples who experience mutual support that strengthens marriages, develops strong families, deepens faith, builds leaders and raises social consciousness.

What Does CFM Offer?

To help married couples in their development, CFM offers its members: a Program of Formation, A Method of Work, and Five Opportunities, which are five means to grow:
  — STUDY of the reality and values of marriage and family life by means of dialogue and exchange of experience.
  — ACTION. As a result of the discussion of the theme, the small groups should come to a commitment of action.
  — FELLOWSHIP. It helps to develop in the couples a spirit of friendship and openness with all by giving and receiving hospitality in group meetings, retreats, encounters and workshops.
  — FINANCIAL RESPONSIBILITY. It promotes the understanding of the Christian value of material goods and the social responsibility in the use of these goods.
  — PRAYER AND LITURGICAL LIFE. It provides and fosters a rich spiritual life so that marriages and families become a community of worship and evangelization.

For more information: CFM National Office
P.O. Box 272
Ames, Iowa 50010.

MARRIAGE ENCOUNTER

Would you and your spouse enjoy a special weekend, alone in a quiet atmosphere, taking the time to share deeply the joy of marriage? If your answer is "yes," then you deserve a Marriage Encounter Weekend.

What's Marriage Encounter?

- A unique opportunity for you to pause and sincerely consider the most important area of your lives . . . your marriage.
- A challenge for you to develop more fully your potential for growth in love, wholeness, holiness and happiness, as you live out God's vision and plan for your marriage each day of your lives.
- A series of presentations and informal talks, given by one of three team couples and a clergy person. Presentations are intensely personal and testimonial. Their purpose is to inspire the couples making the Encounter to become aware of their own lived experiences about their marriage. The second step is exchanging their personal living experiences privately with each other, through the conjugal dialogue. The team's purpose is merely to set the atmosphere. Actually, husband and wife give the Encounter to each other.
- Marriage Encounter weekends are being celebrated all over. If you are interested in experiencing it, you will easily find the way to do it. Try it, and you never will forget this exciting experience.

What The Couples Say?

- "After eight years of marriage and six children we fell in love. Maybe we fell in love again, maybe it was for the first time; it doesn't matter. What does matter is that since we made the M.E. Weekend our lives together have taken on a new meaning."
- "I was looking for a way to share the real me with my husband — my longings, frustrations, goals — but I didn't know how. I feel now we've made a new beginning."
- "I suddenly realized my wife is a mystery. I am discovering her in dialogue, and know that this is a life-long process — to grow in understanding of each other."
- "We have fallen in love again and feel closer than we have ever before."

MARRIAGE RETORNO

If both of you, as a married couple, are longing for a kind of spiritual enrichment, Marriage Retorno could be the answer.

WHAT'S MARRIAGE RETORNO?

- A weekend experience intended for married couples who wish to expand a sense of communion with one another and the Lord.
- A turning to God as a couple. Retorno is a spanish word which means conversion. It is a growth experience which provides married couples the opportunity to turn to God, for the enhancement of their relationship with God.
- A deepening experience of couple spirituality, and prayer as a couple.

WHAT DO COUPLES SAY?

- "We were not praying together. We had a separate way of experiencing faith. Since she is an extrovert and I'm an introvert, we had our own way of praying. Marriage Retorno has been a process for us of becoming more trusting in the Lord and in each other."
- "We had a healthy marriage. We had the grace to work through our ups and downs together, but there was always an unconscious fear of letting go to the point of being open enough to care . . . to be open and vulnerable in prayer. Through Marriage Retorno, the Lord helped us to be confident so that we can expose ourselves to each other with some of our deep fears or woundedness from our past. Now we go to the Lord together and are enriched by a broadening of our faith."
- "We had both taken stabs at reading the Bible before, but this was the first time outside the liturgies we had ever used the Bible for prayer, either individually or as a couple. That was a whole new awakening, that we could let the Scriptures speak to us without knowing the historical background or explanations."
- "We are now beginning to realize what the words conversion and commitment mean to us. Because of couple prayer, these words no longer frighten us, but become a challenge for a more peaceful and joyous living."
- "We made a deeper commitment to God and each other through our commitment to read the Bible every day."

MARRIAGE LITERATURE

Following you will find some recommended books and magazines for your continued marriage enrichment.

- CREATIVE MARRIAGE by Mel Krantzler.
  How to sustain happiness through living together.
- CREATIVE COUPLES by Wallace & Juanita Denton.
  The growth factor in marriage.
- HOW TO HAVE A HAPPY MARRIAGE by David & Vera Mace. A marriage workbook to achieve maturity in marriage.
- THE ART OF STAYING HAPPILY MARRIED by Robert W. Burns, D.S.T. Tested truth from practical experiences.
- THE SECRET OF STAYING IN LOVE by John Powell. S.J. Insights on self-awareness, personal growth and communication.
- WHEN YOUR MARRIAGE GOES STALE by James & Mary Kenny. A concrete assistance in pinpointing trouble spots and developing strategies.
- THE ART OF LOVING by Eric Fromm.
  Love is the answer to the problem of human existence.
- LOVE by Leo Buscaglia.
  Personal reflections on love as the creative force of change.
- LOVERS IN MARRIAGE by Louis Evely.
  A fine collection of essays for married couples.
- STRIKE THE ORIGINAL MATCH by Charles R. Swindoll.
  For rekindling and preserving your marriage fire.
- A JOYFUL MEETING by Mike and Joyce Grace
  A warm and tender, yet factual exploration of marital sexuality.
- 44 HOURS TO CHANGE YOUR LIFE by Henry P. Dunking.
  The story of the M.E. weekend that Henry and his wife lived.
- THE MARRIAGE ENCOUNTER EXPERIENCE by Jeffrey Ventura. Living and encouraging testimonies.
- MARRIAGE ENCOUNTER by Don Demarest, Jerry & Marilyn Sexton. A step-by-step 44-hour Encounter.
- FINDING INTIMACY by Herbert G. Zerof.
  The art of Happiness in living together.
- PERMANENT LOVE by Edward E. Ford & Steven Englund.
- CLOSE COMPANIONS by Dr. David R. Mace.
  A marriage enrichment handbook.
- STRANGERS, LOVERS, FRIENDS by Urban G. Steinmetz.
  An upbeat, positive book for the very-married.
- REBUILDING by Bruce Fisher, Ed. D.
  A warm, experienced guide for when your relationship ends.

- HELPING COUPLES CHANGE by Dr. Richard B. Stuart.
  A social learning approach to marital therapy.
- WALKING IN OLD SHOES by Raymond E. Runde, Ph.D.
  Reflections on how love is comfortable.
- SIMPLE GIFTS by John Kotre.
  The lives of Pat and Patty Crowley, founders of C.F.M.
- YOUR MARRIAGE: THE GREAT ADVENTURE by Gary &
  Kay Atchison. A 12-meeting program for small groups of couples.

Many of these books are available through International Marriage Encounter, 955 Lake Drive, St. Paul, MN 55120. (612) 454-6434.

MAGAZINES

+ MARRIAGE ENCOUNTER

A monthly inside look at the positive side of marriage and family life.

Marriage Encounter Magazine
955 Lake Drive, St. Paul, Minnesota 55120

+ MARRIAGE RETORNO

A quarterly journal of couple prayer and marriage spirituality.
Marriage Retorno Journal
2002 Cheshire Drive, St. Mary's, Ohio 45995.